T0115100

HAMMERIN' HANK
GREENBERG
THE JEWISH BABE RUTH

ADAM PFEFFER

iUniverse, Inc.
Bloomington

HAMMERIN' HANK GREENBERG
THE JEWISH BABE RUTH

iUniverse books may be ordered through booksellers or by contacting:

iUniverse
1663 Liberty Drive
Bloomington, IN 47403
www.iuniverse.com
1-800-Authors (1-800-288-4677)

ISBN: 978-1-4759-7382-2 (sc)
ISBN: 978-1-4759-7383-9 (e)

Printed in the United States of America

iUniverse rev. date: 1/28/2013

There was nobody in the history of the game who took more abuse than Greenberg, unless it was Jackie Robinson…I was there with Hank when it was happening and I heard it. However, Hank was not only equal to it, he was superior to most of the people who were yelling at him. And in the case of Jackie Robinson, Jackie had no place to go after a ball game and Greenberg could go anyplace in the world. Greenberg had to bear that terrible burden on the field, Jackie had to bear it all his life. I wasn't in the National League with Jackie, but I was with Hank and Hank consistently took more abuse than anybody I had ever known.

BIRDIE TEBBETTS, a Detroit teammate for seven seasons

BOOKS BY ADAM PFEFFER

Published by iUniverse:

KOLAK OF THE WEREBEASTS

TWILIGHT OF THE GODS

THE MISSING LINK

TO CHANGE THE WORLD and OTHER STORIES

THE DAY THE DREAM CAME TRUE and OTHER POEMS

THE VISITORS

THE CREATION OF GOD

THE AMAZING SLICK MCKINLEY: GREATEST ATHLETE EVER

THE FANTASTIC FLYING MAN

THE GENIUS WITH THE 225 IQ

30 GREAT STORIES FOR OUR CENTURY

WILD TALES

HAMMERIN' HANK GREENBERG: THE JEWISH BABE RUTH

HANK GREENBERG

GREENBERG, HENRY BENJAMIN
(Hammerin' Hank) BR TR 6'3" 210 lbs.

B. Jan. 1, 1911, New York, N.Y.

1936 Broken wrist. 1941-45 Military Service

Hall of Fame 1956.

	G	AB	H	2B	3B	HR	HRPCT	R	RBI	BB	SO	BA	SA	G by POS
DET A														
1930	1	1	0	0	0	0	0.0	0	0	0	0	.000	.000	
1933	117	449	135	33	3	12	2.7	59	87	46	78	.301	.468	1B-117
1934	153	593	201	**63**	7	26	4.4	118	139	63	93	.339	.600	1B-153
1935	152	619	203	46	16	**36**	5.8	121	**170**	87	91	.328	.628	1B-152
1936	12	46	16	6	2	1	2.2	10	16	9	6	.348	.630	1B-12
1937	154	594	200	49	14	40	6.7	137	**183**	102	101	.337	.668	1B-154
1938	155	556	175	23	4	**58**	10.4	**144**	146	**119**	92	.315	.683	1B-155
1939	138	500	156	42	7	33	6.6	112	112	91	**95**	.312	.622	1B-136
1940	148	573	195	**50**	8	**41**	7.2	129	**150**	93	75	.340	**.670**	OF-148
1941	19	67	18	5	1	2	3.0	12	12	16	12	.269	.463	OF-19
1945	78	270	84	20	2	13	4.8	47	60	42	40	.311	.544	OF-72
1946	142	523	145	29	5	**44**	**8.4**	91	**127**	80	88	.277	.604	1B-140
PIT N														
1947	125	402	100	13	2	25	6.2	71	74	**104**	73	.249	.478	1B-119
TOTALS														
13 Y.	1394	5193	1628	379	71	331	6.4	1051	1276	852	844	.313	.605	1B-1138 OF-239

58 SB   Pinch Hit AB 16   H 3   13 years in the major leagues.

WORLD SERIES RECORD

	G	AB	H	2B	3B	HR	HRPCT	R	RBI	BB	SO	BA	SA	G by POS
DET A														
1934	7	28	9	2	1	1	3.6	4	7	4	9	.321	.571	1B-7
1935	2	6	1	0	0	1	16.7	1	2	1	0	.167	.667	1B-2
1940	7	28	10	2	1	1	3.6	5	6	2	5	.357	.607	OF-7
1945	7	23	7	3	0	2	8.7	7	7	6	5	.304	.696	OF-7
TOTALS														
4YRS.	23	85	27	7	2	5	5.9	17	22	13	19	.318	.624	OF-14

1B-9 1 SB   Did Not Pinch Hit (All **Bold** Numbers- Led the League)

EXT. BASEBALL STADIUM -- DAY

At an unidentified ball park in Major League Baseball's American League, there is a tall man, 23 years old and about 6 foot 4 inches and 215 pounds, standing at the plate right-handed wearing a Detroit Tigers' road uniform with the number five on the back. He takes a few practice swings with three bats before walking up to the plate and waiting for the pitcher to deliver the ball. There are fans sitting in the stands screaming at him from behind.

AN UNIDENTIFIED FAN

Jew bastard.

ANOTHER UNIDENTIFIED FAN

Kike son of a bitch.

The pitcher throws the ball and Hank Greenberg swings. There is a boom and the ball sails long and far into the left field seats. Greenberg runs around the bases with the fans cheering and booing his feat. He shakes hands with the third-base coach and then steps on home plate, shaking hands with the next Tiger hitter, Goose Goslin.

GOOSE GOSLIN

Way to go, Hank.

Hank Greenberg trots to the dugout where the manager, Mickey Cochrane, greets him.

MICKEY COCHRANE

Nice job, Hank.

HANK GREENBERG VOICEOVER

My name is Henry Benjamin Greenberg. I played baseball for the Detroit Tigers of the American League in 1934. It was my second full year with the club and we were winning like those teams with Ty Cobb. I was born in Greenwich Village in New York City on January 1, 1911. My family was Jewish. Orthodox Jewish. My religion was baseball...

He shakes hands with his fellow players and then sits down on the dugout bench next to a young player.

> TIGER PLAYER
>
> That was some shot, Hank.

> HANK GREENBERG
>
> Thanks, it felt pretty good.

> TIGER PLAYER
>
> Hank, people tell me you're Jewish, but I can't believe it.

> HANK GREENBERG
>
> Why?

> TIGER PLAYER
>
> Because I heard all Jews have horns in their head, like the devil.

> HANK GREENBERG
>
> They were lying to you.

> TIGER PLAYER
>
> I don't know about that.

> HANK GREENBERG
>
> Well, check my head. Do you see any horns?

> TIGER PLAYER
>
> You sure you're Jewish?

HANK GREENBERG

Yeah, I'm sure.

TIGER PLAYER

I don't know about that. They tell me a
lot of things about them Jews.

HANK GREENBERG

Well, they're all lies, understand?

TIGER PLAYER

How can they all be lies?

HANK GREENBERG

It's not true.

TIGER PLAYER

You callin' my mama a liar?

HANK GREENBERG

No, I'm just telling you I never heard of it.

MAN IN SUIT

Greenberg, Mr. Navin wants you in his office after the game.

HANK GREENBERG

Fine with me.

TIGER PLAYER

You gonna call Mr. Navin a liar?

HANK GREENBERG

If I have to.

HANK GREENBERG VOICEOVER

We were playing pretty well that year in 1934. If we played
our cards right, we would head right to the World Series. But
sometimes there are more important matters. Like the Jewish
High Holy Days, Rosh Hashanah and Yom Kippur. I already
said my religion was baseball, but somehow I felt like I had an
obligation to Judaism. I had to decide whether to play or not and
it wasn't an easy decision. A prominent Jewish player had never
sat out on a Jewish holiday before. I wanted to be the first.

INT. MR. NAVIN'S OFFICE -- DAY

Greenberg walks in with his Tiger uniform on. The secretary waves
him to Mr. Navin's office. Frank Navin, an old man, is owner of the
Detroit Tigers baseball team.

NAVIN

Come in.

HANK GREENBERG

Hello, Mr. Navin.

NAVIN

Hello, Hank, you should have taken a shower first.

HANK GREENBERG

They said to come right after the game.

Adam Pfeffer

NAVIN

Yes, oh, yes.

HANK GREENBERG

They said it was important.

NAVIN

And it is, Hank.

HANK GREENBERG

Yes, Mr. Navin?

NAVIN

Well, Hank, we're in the pennant race for the first time
in many years. Thanks to you and your teammates.

HANK GREENBERG

We wouldn't have it any other way, Mr. Navin.

NAVIN (smiling)

Yes, but Hank, you know we need you.

HANK GREENBERG

Thank you, Mr. Navin.

NAVIN

So I hope you're not thinking of leaving the team.

HANK GREENBERG

What do you mean?

NAVIN

I mean this whole Jewish New Year thing.

HANK GREENBERG

Well, I'm not supposed to play ball.

NAVIN

Yes, yes, but we're in the middle of a pennant race.

HANK GREENBERG VOICEOVER

I knew he was right. We were only four games ahead of the New York Yankees in September of 1934. Suppose I stayed out of the game and we lost the pennant by one game? Did I want to keep the boys out of the World Series after they had worked so hard? Would that be justice? What would they think and what would the city of Detroit think?

INT. A SYNAGOGUE -- DAY

RABBI

I have been looking at the Talmud and it says the start of the new year is supposed to be a happy day.

REPORTER

Then you think Greenberg should play?

RABBI

I'm not saying that. I'm just saying that Jews in history have played games on that day in celebration of the new year.

REPORTER

What if Greenberg plays baseball for the Tigers?

RABBI

I think it would be perfectly all right to play baseball
if one was not going to go to temple.

REPORTER

Then are you saying it is permissible for Greenberg to play?

RABBI

That he will have to decide for himself.

EXT. BRONX, NEW YORK – DAY 1924

TEN YEARS EARLIER

SARAH GREENBERG

Mrs. Greenberg has such nice children, they tell
me. Too bad one of them has to be a bum.

HANK GREENBERG

Aw, Momma, I love playing baseball.

SARAH GREENBERG

Why are you wasting your time playing baseball? It's a bum's game.

HANK GREENBERG

It makes me feel good, Momma. Like I'm not a freak.

SARAH GREENBERG

Freak? You're big and tall, Henry, that's no crime.

HANK GREENBERG

That's what you say, Momma. But everyone teases me all the time. "How's the air up there?" they say or "My God, look how much he's grown! He's grown two feet in a week." But when I'm on the baseball field, Momma, I'm not a freak anymore. I'm just a big, strong guy who can tear the cover off the ball. This is what I was meant to do, Momma.

SARAH GREENBERG

You'll grow out of this need for baseball in time, Henry. You'll become a doctor, or a dentist, or a lawyer, or a schoolteacher. Then no one will think of you as a freak.

HANK GREENBERG

I want to play baseball, Momma. It's a good game, Momma. You have to be big and fast and then when you hit the ball, you can amaze everyone by your strength and ability.

SARAH GREENBERG

Amaze everyone by your brain, Henry.

HANK GREENBERG

No one wants a big, strong Jew with a brain, Momma.

SARAH GREENBERG

So you're going to play that bum's game instead.

HANK GREENBERG

I'm getting good, Momma. My feet don't get in the way anymore. I'm starting to learn how to play the game, Momma.

Adam Pfeffer

SARAH GREENBERG

Bum's game.

HANK GREENBERG

I'm not a bum when I step onto that field, Momma. I'm not
a bum and I'm not a freak. Not when I go out on that field
and hit that ball, Momma. No, then I'm a champion.

HANK GREENBERG VOICEOVER

Momma never really did understand about baseball. That is,
until the Tigers offered me $9,000 to play. But that feeling about
being a freak of some kind was still there. It was because I was
one of the only Jewish players in baseball. I remember when I
was in the minor leagues, in Raleigh, just standing there on the
field when I realized someone was walking around me, staring.

EXT. BASEBALL STADIUM – DAY

Hank Greenberg is standing on the baseball field when he notices
another player walking around him, staring.

HANK GREENBERG

What're you looking at?

PLAYER

Nothing.

HANK GREENBERG

What do you mean, nothing?

PLAYER

I've never seen a Jew before. I'm just looking.

GREENBERG watches as the player continues to walk around him.

HANK GREENBERG

See anything interesting?

PLAYER

I don't understand it. You look just like anybody else.

HANK GREENBERG

Thanks.

HANK GREENBERG VOICEOVER

I had heard stories from other Jewish players trying to make it to the Major Leagues. One was Andy Cohen, who kept his name, and was an infielder with the New York Giants in the 1920s. He told me when he was playing in the minor leagues in Louisville, Kentucky, a guy in the stands kept shouting, "Christ killer." Andy said he hollered, 'Christ killer this' and 'Christ killer that' and he finally got sick of it. He ended up taking a bat and going to the stands. Looking up at the guy, he shouted, "Yeah, come down here and I'll kill you, too." That's what baseball was like in those days. You had big country kids and tough city boys together looking for a better life.

INT. A SYNAGOGUE – DAY

RABBI

I think you should think this over very carefully, Henry.

HANK GREENBERG

I only want to do the right thing, rabbi.

RABBI

The question is will anybody understand if
you do choose to do the right thing.

HANK GREENBERG

I can make a statement of some kind.

RABBI

Yes, a lot of people would know, but Henry
you have to do what's right for you.

HANK GREENBERG

I'm still not sure what the right thing to do really is.

RABBI

Whatever you decide will be the right thing, Henry.

EXT. NAVIN FIELD, DETROIT – DAY

HANK GREENBERG is sitting on the Tiger bench, looking gloomily at his teammates. He glances at a copy of that morning's Detroit Free Press with the headline, Happy New Year, Hank. ELDEN

AUKER, that day's starting pitcher for the Tigers, is talking to a reporter as Hank makes his way to the clubhouse.

ELDEN AUKER

I didn't know what Rosh Hashanah was. The papers said Hank wasn't going to play because it was a Jewish holiday. That's when I found out what Rosh Hashanah was. He didn't take batting practice. I was a little upset because I thought I'm going to pitch a ball game without Hank. He is pretty important to us.

REPORTER

Did you know Hank was Jewish?

ELDEN AUKER

I came from Kansas and I never knew what a Jew was. Never gave it a thought. I would say Hank was the first Jewish person I ever met. The Jewish people aren't in Kansas. And I never looked at Hank any other way except just like a guy looks at the rest of the guys. So all I know is, I hope Hank will play.

REPORTER

He's pretty important to this team, isn't he?

ELDEN AUKER

He sure is. He's our first baseman and we need him.

HANK GREENBERG walks into the clubhouse and begins undressing. He sits there in his t-shirt and pants just staring and thinking. MARV OWEN, the Tiger third baseman, walks into the clubhouse and sees Greenberg sitting there.

MARV OWEN

What the hell is the matter with you, you sick?

Adam Pfeffer

HANK GREENBERG

No.

MARV OWEN

You know I heard all about this Rosh Hashanah thing.

HANK GREENBERG

Yeah, yeah.

MARV OWEN

Is something bothering you?

HANK GREENBERG

I don't know what to do.

MARV OWEN

You gotta play ball, that's what you gotta do.

HANK GREENBERG

No, it's one of my church holidays.

MARV OWEN

They're not in a pennant race.

HANK GREENBERG

Look, I can't explain it. I'll just have to decide for myself.

MARV OWEN

Hank, I got an idea. We're going to be out there for twenty
minutes for batting practice. The first thing that comes
to your mind, do it. If it says, play — you play. If it says
don't play — don't play. You'll make the right decision.

MARV OWEN walks out of the locker room, leaving HANK GREENBERG to sit there and think.

                    RADIO ANNOUNCER'S VOICE
What a glorious day for a ball game, ladies and gentlemen.
The Detroit Tigers, led by the G-Men of baseball, Greenberg,
Gehringer and Goslin, will take on the Boston Red Sox in an
afternoon affair that has had its share of controversy. Hank
Greenberg, the star first baseman for the Tigers and Jewish,
has to decide whether to play for his team in the thick of a
pennant race or sit out as prescribed by most of his religion…

The Tiger team has just finished batting practice and is walking back to the locker room. They see HANK GREENBERG with his uniform on smiling.

                    HANK GREENBERG
                    I'm going to play.

                    MICKEY COCHRANE
That's fantastic, Hank, we knew you'd make the right decision.

                    HANK GREENBERG
                    My teammates come first.

                    ELDEN AUKER
              That's Hank for you, I told you.

EXT. NAVIN FIELD – DAY

The Tigers are playing the Boston Red Sox on Rosh Hashanah.

Adam Pfeffer

RADIO ANNOUNCER'S VOICE

The Red Sox are leading this game, one to nothing, as Hank
Greenberg steps into the box in the seventh inning. The big
first baseman is playing today's game even though many in
his Jewish religion believe he shouldn't be out there on the
ball field. Greenberg's reply was that his teammates were
more important than his religion and therefore decided to
don the uniform. Here's the pitch from Gordon Rhodes.
It's a long fly into left field, way back there, that ball is gone,
ladies and gentlemen. A mighty blow over the scoreboard
with room to spare, Happy New Year, Hank Greenberg!

We see HANK GREENBERG, number five, trotting around the
bases in his home Tiger uniform. The fans are all cheering and his
teammates congratulate him as he trots into the dugout.

MICKEY COCHRANE

Happy Rosh Hashanah, boys.

MARV OWEN

What a shot, Hank, baby.

A shot of the ballpark with the Tigers up at bat against the Red
Sox.

RADIO ANNOUNCER'S VOICE

We've come to the bottom of the ninth inning with the Tigers and
Red Sox tied at one. Coming up for the Tigers is their slugging
first baseman Hank Greenberg. Hank tied up the game in the
seventh with a mighty homer over the scoreboard. Hank digs in
at the plate and waits for Rhodes to throw the pitch. It's high and
outside for ball one. Hank almost didn't make it to the ballpark
today because of the Jewish holiday Rosh Hashanah. Here's the
pitch and what a smash. It's sailing down the line for a home run.
Hank Greenberg has won the game he almost didn't play in!

People are rushing onto the field as Greenberg trots around the bases.

UNIDENTIFIED FAN

What a shot.

ANOTHER UNIDENTIFIED FAN

Yeah, he's Jewish all right, the Jewish Babe Ruth.

RADIO ANNOUNCER'S VOICE

The traditional tenacity of the world's oldest and
most beleaguered people today had played its part
in a pennant race – winning a ball game.

Greenberg is mobbed by his teammates at home plate after rounding the bases.

RADIO ANNOUNCER'S VOICE

There was more than the mighty bone and sinew of Hank
Greenberg behind those two home runs which went whistling
out of Navin Field…They were propelled by a force born of the
desperation and pride of a young Jew who turned his back on
the ancient ways of his race and creed to help his teammates.

INT. NAVIN FIELD LOCKER ROOM – DAY

GREENBERG is mobbed by his Tiger teammates as they get dressed in the locker room with the newspaper reporters surrounding them.

Adam Pfeffer

ELDEN AUKER

I knew God would be on our side today.

MARV OWEN

Hammerin' Hank, that's what they're calling him.

A REPORTER

Have anything to say, Hank?

HANK GREENBERG

The good Lord did not let me down.

MICKEY COCHRANE

You can say that again.

ELDEN AUKER

How do you say it, Hank?

HANK GREENBERG

Good Yontif.

ELDEN AUKER

Yeah, good *yontif.*

CHARLIE GEHRINGER

That goes for me, too.

The players laugh as they celebrate the victory.

INT. NAVIN FIELD LOCKER ROOM
THE NEXT DAY – DAY

MARV OWEN walks into the locker room and sees GREENBERG
in his Tiger home uniform brooding.

> MARV OWEN
>
> Goddamnit, Hank, you won the ball game
> with two home runs, what's wrong?

> HANK GREENBERG
>
> When I got back to my hotel my phone rang half the
> night. I caught hell from my fellow parishioners, I caught
> hell from some rabbis, and I don't know what to do,
> it's ten days until the next holiday – Yom Kippur.

> MARV OWEN
>
> Don't worry, when it comes you'll make the
> right decision like you did yesterday.

> HANK GREENBERG
>
> But you don't understand, Yom Kippur is the day
> of atonement, the most sacred holiday of the year
> for Jews. I just can't let them down again.

> MARV OWEN
>
> Who said you let anybody down? A lot of your
> people root for this team, right, Hank?

> HANK GREENBERG
>
> Yeah, but…

> MARV OWEN
>
> Well, you didn't let down the Tigers, I can tell you that.

The two of them walk out of the locker room and onto the field. There are people screaming from the other dugout.

UNIDENTIFIED PLAYER

Pants presser.

ANOTHER UNIDENTIFIED PLAYER

Let's see what you've got, you big Jew.

A reporter is interviewing MICKEY COCHRANE, the Tiger manager.

REPORTER

Some say the Tigers have the American League
pennant signed, sealed and delivered—

MICKEY COCHRANE

You never know what's going to happen.

REPORTER

Then you think Hank should play on Yom Kippur?

MICKEY COCHRANE

That's going to be up to him.

REPORTER

Many people say he's the most important cog on
the team. He's hitting .338 with 25 homers—

MICKEY COCHRANE

He's very important to us, but if Hank decides he has
to sit out the game because of his religion, then that's
all right with me and the Tiger organization.

INT. THE HOME OF HANK GREENBERG'S PARENTS – DAY

Newspaper reporters are inside the home of David and Sarah Greenberg, Hank Greenberg's father and mother.

DAVID GREENBERG

We are an Orthodox family. He promised us when we saw him in Philadelphia on Detroit's last trip to the East that he would not play on Rosh Hashanah or Yom Kippur.

REPORTER

Are you angry Hank played?

DAVID GREENBERG

He wrote us later that he was sorry he had played on Rosh Hashanah, but Mickey Cochrane said he was needed and Henry could not refuse very well.

SARAH GREENBERG

It's not so terrible, either. I see young men go to the temple in the morning and then maybe do worse things than Henry did.

DAVID GREENBERG

Yom Kippur is different. I will put my foot down and Henry will obey.

REPORTER

Will you be very angry if he plays again?

DAVID GREENBERG

This is between Henry and God.

Adam Pfeffer

REPORTER
Do you think God roots for the Tigers?

DAVID GREENBERG
Is there any other team?

The reporters laugh at DAVID GREENBERG's remark.

HANK GREENBERG VOICEOVER
Well, I was determined to make the right decision. This time,
it was a bit easier. I had already played for my teammates
on Rosh Hashanah. How could they argue with my decision
to honor my religion on Yom Kippur? There was no doubt
we were still going to have a tough time before winning the
pennant We were scheduled to play the second-place New
York Yankees. It would be a tough game but how could
taking off Yom Kippur really hurt us? Wouldn't we gain
a fan that was more important than any other fan in the
world? Could it hurt to please the big slugger in the sky?

EXT. A DETROIT STREET – DAY

A crowd of people in suits and dresses are walking down a street
in Detroit.

A MAN IN A SUIT AND YARMULKE
Good *Yontif,* Mr. Greenberg.

HANK GREENBERG
Good *Yontif.*

A BOY IN A SUIT AND YARMULKE
Hank, do you think God is a Tigers fan?

HANK GREENBERG (smiling)
I can't really say.

BOY IN SUIT AND YARMULKE
Bet he is now.

HANK GREENBERG
Maybe.

They walk to the Shaarey Zedek synagogue and step inside. The rabbi and the congregation are praying as HANK GREENBERG walks down the aisle. The congregation is sitting down and suddenly, everyone starts looking at Greenberg. They now start applauding and give him a standing ovation.

HANK GREENBERG
Thank you, everyone. Good *Yontif.*

HANK GREENBERG VOICEOVER
I was embarrassed; I didn't know what to do. It was a tremendous ovation for a kid who was only twenty-three years old, and in a synagogue, no less. When I was playing I used to resent being singled out as a Jewish ballplayer, period. I'm not sure why or when I changed, because I'm still not a particularly religious person. Later in life, though, I found myself wanting to be remembered not only as a great ballplayer, but even more as a great Jewish ballplayer. Anyway, we went on to win the pennant in 1934, the first time the Tigers had won a pennant in twenty-five years. The only game I missed that year was the game on Yom Kippur. I'm not sorry about that. The World Series against the St. Louis Cardinals was another matter altogether.

EXT. NAVIN FIELD – DAY

The Detroit Tigers and the St. Louis Cardinals are on the field for the 1934 World Series.

RADIO ANNOUNCER

Welcome to this first radio broadcast of the World Series, ladies and gentlemen. This year's Series pits the "Gashouse Gang" against the "G-Men." The Cardinals are led by manager and second baseman Frankie Frisch and Ducky Medwick in left. The stars of the pitching corps are the Dean brothers, Dizzy and Daffy...

HANK GREENBERG is walking away from batting practice when he sees DIZZY DEAN.

DIZZY DEAN

Hello, Mose.

HANK GREENBERG

What do you want, Dean?

DIZZY DEAN

Ain't you heard Ol' Diz is pitching today?

HANK GREENBERG

What difference does that make to me?

DIZZY DEAN

We'll see, Mose, we'll see.

RADIO ANNOUNCER

The Cardinals are leading as we go to the bottom of the eighth inning. Dean is still on the mound as Hank Greenberg comes up to the plate. Greenberg has already singled in the sixth. Greenberg grabs three bats and then discards two of them. He steps up to the plate and waits for the pitch. He takes a mighty swing and the ball soars into the bleachers in Navin Field. A home run for Hank Greenberg and now the Cardinals lead the first game of the World Series, 8 to 3.

We see Greenberg rounding the bases and being congratulated by his teammates.

MARV OWEN (shouting at Dean on the mound)
Hello, Mose.

CHARLIE GEHRINGER
I guess Moses played at first base, right, Hank?

HANK GREENBERG
Can't really say, Charlie.

CHARLIE GEHRINGER
Well, Ol' Diz seems to know.

HANK GREENBERG
I wouldn't be surprised if his ancestor was the Pharoah.

RADIO ANNOUNCER
And so the Cardinals take the first game of the World Series behind the pitching of DIZZY DEAN. They capitalized on five errors by the Tigers' infield as Ducky Medwick led the attack with four hits…

DIZZY DEAN is on the field surrounded by reporters.

DIZZY DEAN

I got a kick out of pitching to Greenberg. He couldn't see my fastball so I tells Frankie Frisch that I wanted to see this feller hit one. I'd heard tell he was some shakes as a batter so I gave him one where he liked it. He cow tailed it, too.

REPORTER

So you let him hit it, Diz?

DIZZY DEAN

Anybody could have hit that ball for a home run.
Our clubhouse boy could have done it.

The reporters laughed.

LEO DUROCHER

Greenberg got that homer off a curve that didn't break. Diz was just tired after a big season.

RADIO ANNOUNCER

Join us tomorrow, ladies and gentlemen, for game two of the 1934 World Series when the pitchers will be Bill Hallahan and Schoolboy Rowe…

HANK GREENBERG VOICEOVER

Ol' Diz and the rest of the Cardinal team had a hard time intimidating me. I was a city boy from the Bronx and Greenwich Village and I took my hitting seriously.

EXT. CROTONA PARK, THE BRONX –
DAY 1927 SEVEN YEARS EARLIER

PAT MCDONALD is throwing the shot put in the outfield at Crotona Park. HANK GREENBERG hits a ball that bounces toward him. He bends down and picks up the ball. GREENBERG comes to retrieve the ball.

PAT MCDONALD

Son, you know who I am?

HANK GREENBERG

You won a gold medal in the Olympics.

PAT MCDONALD

Yeah, I know something about sports.

HANK GREENBERG

I'm sure you do, seeing how you throw
that thing (shot put) around.

PAT MCDONALD

I've seen you hitting those balls at the park many times.

HANK GREENBERG

We didn't mean to get in your way or anything.

PAT MCDONALD

Well, I might have gotten upset a few times.

HANK GREENBERG

I'm just trying to perfect my swing.

Adam Pfeffer

PAT MCDONALD

Yes, well about your swing, I just came back from
watching the New York Yankees play baseball.

HANK GREENBERG

They're a swell team.

PAT MCDONALD

Yes, but I was watching them.

HANK GREENBERG

You must have enjoyed it.

PAT MCDONALD

Now just wait a minute. I wanted to tell you that I
just came from watching the Yankees play and, by
God, you hit a ball better than Lou Gehrig.

HANK GREENBERG (smiling)

Well, that's the greatest compliment I ever had, Mr. McDonald.

HANK GREENBERG VOICEOVER

And it was, too. I lived only a few miles from Yankee Stadium,
but up until that point, it never entered into my head that
I had anything in common with Major Leaguers. And now,
this man, this Pat McDonald, was telling me I hit the ball as
hard as one of the great stars of the game. So how could Ol'
Dizzy Dean and the St. Louis Cardinals intimidate me?

EXT. ST. LOUIS BASEBALL STADIUM – DAY 1934

RADIO ANNOUNCER

Hammerin' Hank Greenberg has broken out of his slump,
going 4 for 5 today as the Tigers evened the Series, two
games apiece. Greenberg had three RBI's as the Tigers belted
out thirteen hits and ten runs against Cardinal pitching...

EXT. NAVIN FIELD – DAY

The Tigers are gathered in the locker room
in their home white uniforms.

MICKEY COCHRANE

Okay, guys, this is it, the seventh game.

CHARLIE GEHRINGER

We'll beat Ol' Diz today.

MICKEY COCHRANE

Just don't let him get to you.

CHARLIE GEHRINGER

How you feeling, Hank?

HANK GREENBERG

Pretty good.

CHARLIE GEHRINGER

Just wait for your pitch.

GREENBERG walks from the locker room to the dugout. He steps
into the light and sees DIZZY DEAN standing there in the St. Louis
road uniform.

Adam Pfeffer

DIZZY DEAN

Hello, Mose, what makes you so white?
Boy, you're a-shakin' like a leaf.

HANK GREENBERG (smiling)

Go on, get out of here.

DIZZY DEAN

I get it; you done hear that Ol Diz was
goin' to pitch. Well, you're right.

HANK GREENBERG

You don't scare me, you big country yokel.

DIZZY DEAN

Don't worry, Mose, it'll all be over in a few minutes. Old
Diz is goin' to pitch, and he's goin' to pin your ears back.

HANK GREENBERG

Yokel.

DIZZY DEAN

Mose.

HANK GREENBERG VOICEOVER

I don't get easily rattled, but that seventh game of the 1934
World Series was a disaster. I couldn't do anything right that
day, and there was Ol' Diz abusing me every chance he could.

HANK GREENBERG makes an error on a ball at first base.

DIZZY DEAN

Hey, Mose, c'mon in the clubhouse and get your
meal money. You're the best player we got.

RADIO ANNOUNCER

It's been a dreadful day for the Tigers and Hank Greenberg.
But some would say Dizzy Dean's behavior was both vulgar and
unsporting. He was laughing pitching to Greenberg even before
the ball got to the plate. Greenberg fanned three times and Dean
seemed to be having the time of his life. The Cardinals ended up
taking the game and the Series with an 11 to nothing victory...

INT. TIGER LOCKER ROOM – DAY

HANK GREENBERG

Well, Dean made me look like a monkey.

MARV OWEN

It's all right, Hank, we all had a bad game.

HANK GREENBERG

They tell me I swung at a ball two feet
over my head. I don't doubt it.

MICKEY COCHRANE

It was pretty vicious out there. We'll get them next year.

HANK GREENBERG VOICEOVER

Looking back, I didn't have a great Series, but I didn't have a bad
one either. The Cardinals called me everything under the sun.
Anyway, I struck out nine times in seven games, but I also drove

Adam Pfeffer

in seven runs, one short of the record for RBIs in the World Series at the time, and hit .321. Not terrible. I had received only $5,000 for my performance in 1934. The Tigers decided to increase my salary to $15,000 the next year, an awful lot of money for those days and for a twenty-four-year-old man. It was only five years before that I received my first contract...

INT. GREENBERG HOME IN THE BRONX, NEW YORK – DAY 1929 FIVE YEARS EARLIER

HANK GREENBERG

Pop, are you against baseball as a career?

DAVID GREENBERG

The only thing important is your studies, Henry.

HANK GREENBERG

The Tigers offered $9,000.

DAVID GREENBERG whistled softly.

DAVID GREENBERG

$9,000? You mean they want to give you that kind of money just to go out and play with the baseball?

HANK GREENBERG

That's right.

DAVID GREENBERG

And they'll let you finish college first?

HANK GREENBERG
Yes, Pop.

DAVID GREENBERG (sitting down)
I thought baseball was a game. But it's a business
– apparently a very good business.

HANK GREENBERG
So what do you think I should do, Pop?

DAVID GREENBERG
Take the money.

HANK GREENBERG VOICEOVER
I listened to Pop and took the money. But I also tried to go to
college on a scholarship. The Tigers worked it all out. They would
pay me $6,000 for signing and $3,000 when I reported to Detroit
four years later. So I signed the contract and was off to NYU. It
didn't last long. After my first year at college, I decided to go to
the Tigers' camp in Lakeland, Florida and play some baseball...

EXT. NAVIN FIELD – DAY 1935 SIX YEARS LATER

HANK GREENBERG VOICEOVER
We got off to a rousing start in spring of 1935. The team
was in first place early in the race and stayed there. I had a
great first half. I led the league in home runs and believe I set
a record with 110 runs batted in by the All-Star game, but
still I wasn't picked for the American League all-star team.

REPORTER

They picked Gehrig for first base, Hank.

HANK GREENBERG

Gehrig? Well, that's all right.

REPORTER

Are you upset?

HANK GREENBERG

How many RBIs have I got?

REPORTER

Eighty-four

HANK GREENBERG

You're wrong. The number is eighty-five.

How many does Gehrig have? You don't know, eh? Well, he'll be batting for quite a while before he gets up to eighty-five. What do I care about All-Star games, anyway? Let Gehrig have his fun, I want to get to the Series again.

REPORTER

Don't you care about playing in an All-Star game?

HANK GREENBERG

I care all right, but I don't know what I'm going to have to do to beat out Gehrig and Foxx. You see I have a little problem.

REPORTER

What's that, Hank?

HANK GREENBERG

I was born Jewish.

A little girl, about 13 years old, walks over to where GREENBERG
and the reporter are sitting.

A LITTLE GIRL

Mr. Greenberg, you're my knight in shining armor.

HANK GREENBERG

What's your name?

A LITTLE GIRL

Sarah, I'm Jewish. I was pretty disappointed when Max
Baer lost to Jimmy Braddock, but now I'm banking it all
on you, Mr. Greenberg. Please don't fail our people.

HANK GREENBERG

I'll try not to, Sarah. You tell your friends
that Hank won't let you down.

REPORTER

You have an immense responsibility, Hank.

HANK GREENBERG

Yes, I have. I mean you guys rarely mention my name without
"Jewish" or "Hebrew ballplayer" accompanying it.

REPORTER

Well, soon we're going to have put something
else in front of your name.

Adam Pfeffer

HANK GREENBERG
What's that?

REPORTER
Great, as in the great Jewish ballplayer Hank Greenberg.

EXT. NAVIN FIELD – DAY 1935

RADIO ANNOUNCER
Welcome ladies and gentlemen to the 1935 World Series
between the Detroit Tigers and the Chicago Cubs. The weather
couldn't be more perfect with the rain that was here yesterday
long gone. It's a full house here in Detroit, surely one of the
largest crowds to ever witness a ball game in this city.

Inside the Tiger dugout, the players are talking.

MARV OWEN
You really put on a show in batting practice, Hank.

HANK GREENBERG
I'm not going to be intimidated like last year.

Greenberg walks onto the field, grabs three bats, and begins swinging
them. The Cub players are shouting from their dugout.

A CUB PLAYER
Jew son of a bitch.

RADIO ANNOUNCER

Here's Hank Greenberg. He grounded out to third last time up. Wait a minute, Umpire George Moriarty is walking over to the Cubs' bench apparently in response to what they were shouting at Hank Greenberg...

UMPIRE MORIARTY

You wanna play baseball or you wanna scream names?

A CUB PLAYER

What's that Jew doing on the field?

UMPIRE MORIARTY

He's got as much right as any of you.

A CUB PLAYER

We don't have to like it.

UMPIRE MORIARTY

Listen, you mugs, no ballplayer can call me the names you called Greenberg. Anymore profanity and I'm going to chase five of you off the bench with your manager leading the procession.

A CUB PLAYER

What do you care about that Jew bastard?

UMPIRE MORIARTY

I care about fair play, that's all.

A CUB PLAYER

Then why don't you chase that Jew?

UMPIRE MORIARTY

Just hope I don't chase all of you.

As UMPIRE MORIARTY walks back to the plate, the Cub players continue to shout at GREENBERG.

A CUB PLAYER

Throw him a pork chop, he'll never hit it!

A CUB PLAYER

Can't hit that!

A CUB PLAYER

Jewish son of a bitch.

GREENBERG hits a grounder to third and is thrown out at first. He walks back to his dugout while the Cub players are still shouting.

A CUB PLAYER

Go back to the dugout, you big Jew.

HANK GREENBERG VOICEOVER

In those days, they had three or four guys who were supposed to sit in the dugout and ride certain players. I was one of those players who were supposed to be ridiculed. But it wasn't only me, I can tell you that. Phil Cavarretta, the Cubs' first baseman, said teams were riding him, too. He got things like 'you dirty dago' and 'wop' and things like that. It was all what they called, bench jockeying.

RADIO ANNOUNCER

Welcome, ladies and gentlemen, to game two of the 1935 World Series. Well, it's mighty cold out there,

48 degrees at noon. But we're scheduled to play some baseball with Charlie Root taking on Tommy Bridges…

AN UNIDENTIFIED FAN

This is the coldest day for a World Series since 1907. I remember that one all right. The Cubs and the Tigers played in a snowstorm.

RADIO ANNOUNCER

Two runs are already in for the Tigers in this first inning, ladies and gentlemen. Here's Hank Greenberg. He steps up to the plate with Charlie Gehringer on. Here's the pitch. It's a long fly ball to left field, that ball is gone. Hank Greenberg has just put the Tigers ahead, four to nothing, on this cold day in Detroit.

CHARLIE GEHRINGER

Nice shot, Hank

HANK GREENBERG

My pleasure, Charlie.

RADIO ANNOUNCER

We go to the seventh inning, ladies and gentlemen. And Hammerin' Hank Greenberg steps to the plate. Here's the pitch, and it hits Greenberg. Oh my, ladies and gentlemen, there is some fierce shouting from both benches as Greenberg trots on down to first base. Pete Fox now the batter. And there's a single into right field, Greenberg is rounding third and the throw is to second base. Greenberg is now headed for home. Here's the throw, the slide, and Greenberg is hurt. He got mangled at the plate by Gabby Hartnett as he tried to slide in for the run…

HANK GREENBERG VOICEOVER

I ended up finishing the game, but the injury finished me for the rest of the Series. We went on to win that Series in six games. Naturally, I was disappointed that I couldn't play. I was in uniform, but I felt like a stranger on the team I helped to win the pennant. The Series was clinched in Detroit, and the whole city went wild. It was the greatest celebration in the history of Detroit.

INT. THE GREENBERG HOME -- DAY

DAVID GREENBERG

How's your wrist, Henry?

HANK GREENBERG

It'll be okay, Pop.

RADIO ANNOUNCER

Hank Greenberg of the Detroit Tigers has been named the winner of the most valuable player award in the American League. Greenberg was the unanimous choice of the eight representatives of the Baseball Writers Association of America. Wes Ferrell, who had won twenty-five games for the Red Sox, was second. Greenberg had 36 homers, a league-leading 170 RBI's and a .328 batting average.

SARAH GREENBERG

That's wonderful, Henry, you are the best player in the American League.

HANK GREENBERG

Even if it's a bum's game, Momma?

SARAH GREENBERG

Oh, Henry, you're not going to hold that against Momma, are you?

HANK GREENBERG

Of course not, Momma. I just want you to realize
that what you said might not have been correct.

SARAH GREENBERG

Yes, but I was correct about one thing.

DAVID GREENBERG

What's that, Momma?

SARAH GREENBERG

That Henry is the best player in the American League.

DAVID GREENBERG

Yes, Momma, you got that correct all right.

HANK GREENBERG

I got off to a flying start in 1936, hitting around .350 and
leading the league in runs batted in. We were in Washington
in early May, the twelfth game of the season, when Marv
Owen fielded a ground ball at third base. He threw it over
to me at first and I stretched to get the throw. The throw
was fading into the baseline and the batter was Jake Powell.
He ran right into me coming down the line and I broke my
left wrist once again. I was out for the rest of the season. I
knew it was no accident. Powell deliberately ran into me.

EXT. NAVIN FIELD – DAY

HANK GREENBERG, his left wrist in a cast, is in the Tiger locker
room.

Adam Pfeffer

CHARLIE GEHRINGER

Hey, Hank, it's not the same without you.

HANK GREENBERG

Well, the Tigers told me to take it easy
and make sure it heals all right.

MARV OWEN

No, heavy lifting, big guy.

HANK GREENBERG

No, but I'll be back, you can count on that.

CHARLIE GEHRINGER

Man, without you and Cochrane, we're in a heap of trouble.

HANK GREENBERG

Nothing I can do about it this year. But I think
I'll be ready when the season opens.

HANK GREENBERG VOICEOVER

1937 turned out to be my best year. I say this because ballplayers
appreciate that runs batted in are all that's important to a
ball team. It isn't how many doubles or what your batting
average is or how many home runs you hit. The bottom line
is who drives in the runs. And in 1937, I drove in 183 runs.
That was quite an accomplishment. It was one RBI short of
the American League record held by Lou Gehrig, who did
it in 1931, the year after Hack Wilson of the Cubs set the
Major League record of 190, which still stands today. I tried
to break the record, but it came down to the final game
of the season. We were playing Cleveland in Detroit.

EXT. NAVIN FIELD -- DAY

RADIO ANNOUNCER

Welcome to the final game of the year, ladies and gentlemen, with the Cleveland Indians playing the Detroit Tigers. On the mound for the Tribe is Johnny Allen, who is going for a record sixteen wins in a row for a season. Starting for the Tigers is Whistlin' Jake Wade, who was recently called up from the minor leagues...

HANK GREENBERG

Just get on, and I'll knock you in.

CHARLIE GEHRINGER

You got it, Hank.

RADIO ANNOUNCER

Here comes Hank Greenberg with a man on second and one out. Here's the pitch from Johnny Allen and it's a base hit to left field, scoring the runner. Hank Greenberg has 183 runs batted in, ladies and gentlemen...

HANK GREENBERG VOICEOVER

But that's all I would get. Jake Wade pitched a one-hit shutout and beat Johnny Allen, one to nothing. I lost to Lou Gehrig by one run batted in to end the 1937 season. The next season, 1938, I would concentrate on hitting home runs.

RADIO ANNOUNCER

Hammerin' Hank Greenberg is ahead of Babe Ruth's record-setting home run pace after hitting four consecutive homers in Detroit against Washington in a doubleheader. Greenberg belted out two homers in his last two at bats in the first game and then two more in his next at bats in the second game...

HANK GREENBERG VOICEOVER

It was from that point in the season that I began shooting for home runs, chasing the record. The Detroit ball park was the best park for me to hit home runs. It had a good background and the fences were just the right distance for pulling the ball – 340 down the left-field line and then 365 in left-center. It was a good poke to centerfield, about 450 feet from home plate.

EXT. NAVIN FIELD – DAY

Reporters are crowding around Hank Greenberg as he stands on the field near the Tiger dugout.

REPORTER

Hank, what do you think about breaking the record?

HANK GREENBERG

I don't know, boys, you really have to get hot
especially at the end of the season.

REPORTER

How much does it mean to you, Hank, to try to break the record?

HANK GREENBERG

Well, there's a lot going on, boys, like Hitler in Germany. I like to feel that as a Jew, if I hit a home run, I'm hitting one against Hitler.

REPORTER

How about in America, Hank, do you think people will be upset if a Jewish ballplayer breaks the Babe's record?

HANK GREENBERG

I can't worry about that, boys, I'm just trying to show
that there's no difference between any of us. I'm just like
the Babe in many ways, not just in hitting home runs.

REPORTER

Oh, come on, Hank, why don't show everybody your horns?

HANK GREENBERG

Can't right now, I have to go out there
and hit some more home runs.

Everybody is laughing.

REPORTER

Do you think you can do it?

HANK GREENBERG

Funny thing, I've been asked two questions all season. For
the first two months everybody wanted to know when I
would snap out of my slump. Now all I hear is, 'Hank, do
you think you can break Ruth's record of 60 home runs?

REPORTER

And what were the answers, Hank?

HANK GREENBERG

Well, the answers to both questions is the same; I don't
know. I'm not counting on breaking the record and I'm not
letting it bother me. The Babe was the greatest home-run
hitter we ever had, but the best he could do was 60. Only
two others, Foxx and Hack Wilson, hit over 50, so it's pretty
tough for anybody, including myself, to do better than the
best. Seriously, though, if I can keep pace with the record until
September 7, I think I can do it. Babe hit 6 homers that first

week in September, then he tapered off. His season ended a week earlier than mine. With breaks I think I can do it.

HANK GREENBERG VOICEOVER

What made it even tougher to break that record is that nobody wanted me to do it, except for the Jewish fans. You can't really blame them. The Babe was loved by everybody and no one wanted to see a Jew break his cherished record. I decided I would give it a try, though. I would take a lot from the fans and players, but I was on a heck of a pace. I just kept hitting more and more home runs. But, as I said, not everybody was thrilled with my effort. One incident occurred when we were playing the Chicago White Sox...

WHITE SOX PLAYER

Hey, you big Jew.

RADIO ANNOUNCER

Joe Kuhel the batter for the White Sox. There's a base hit to right field and Kuhel stops at first base.

WHITE SOX PLAYER

Come on, Joe, take a big lead on that Jew.

WHITE SOX PLAYER

Slide back into first and spike him, Joe.

The ball is thrown to first base by the pitcher where Joe Kuhel slides back into Greenberg and spikes him.

HANK GREENBERG

Ow, so you wanna play rough?

There's a fight on the field, Greenberg and Kuhel throwing punches. They roll around on the field and then are separated.

UMPIRE

You two guys are out of the game, you understand?

JOE KUHEL

You big Jew.

HANK GREENBERG

This big Jew is going to teach you a lesson
you're never going to forget.

JOE KUHEL

You playing just for the money?

HANK GREENBERG

You better hope they don't pay me to tan your
hide, Kuhel. I'll gladly do it for half the price.

JOE KUHEL

My Mama says you Jews are guilty of the blood libel.

HANK GREENBERG

Who would want your blood or children, Kuhel?

JOE KUHEL

No Jew is going to talk to me like that.

UMPIRE

Don't you guys understand? You're both out of this game.

JOE KUHEL

Jew.

HANK GREENBERG
Redneck.

INT. LOCKER ROOM -- DAY

Hank Greenberg walks to the locker room and begins undressing. In the background, a ball game is being played. When Greenberg is finally dressed in civilian clothes, we hear the players coming back to the locker room. Greenberg walks from the Tiger locker room to the White Sox locker room. When he appears, the players stop what they are doing wondering what Greenberg is going to say.

HANK GREENBERG
The guy that called me a yellow son of a bitch get on
his feet and come up here and call it to my face.

The White Sox players are silent.

HANK GREENBERG
I'm not going to take anymore from you guys, understand?
I've had just about enough. It's true I'm Jewish, but can't we
be human about it? I'm no different than any of you. Got it?

The White Sox players stay silent.

HANK GREENBERG
No one wants to mix it up? Good, maybe
we'll be civil about all this.

The White Sox players say nothing.

HANK GREENBERG

That's all I had to say, gentlemen. I'll be seeing you.
Oh, and the next guy that calls me a Jew of any kind
is going to get it from me. I'm not scared of any of
you mugs. Thank you, gentlemen, for your time.

Greenberg walks out of the White Sox locker room.

WHITE SOX PLAYER (spitting)

He ain't yellow, but he's sure a Jew son of a bitch.

The other White Sox players in the locker room laugh.

HANK GREENBERG VOICEOVER

The American League president, William Harridge, fined me
$50 for that fight with Kuhel. He did, however, criticize 'certain'
White Sox players for what he termed 'unsportsmanlike
conduct and use of insulting and abusive language to members
of the opposing team.' He said he had warned Sox manager
Jimmy Dykes that 'any players found guilty of a repetition of
these tactics will be ejected from the game, with suspension
following.' I still say Kuhel deliberately spiked me sliding
into first base. Anyway, not many took up the challenge of
fighting me. The Kuhel fight was one of the few altercations
I had as a baseball player, and after I gave my explanation to
American League President Harridge, he returned the $50 fine.
Meanwhile, I kept chasing Babe Ruth's home run record of 60.

RADIO ANNOUNCER

Greenberg's present pace is ahead of Babe Ruth's.
Ruth hit his 33rd of the year in the Yankees' 95th game.
Greenberg's 33rd came in Detroit's 88th game.

HANK GREENBERG VOICEOVER

Only three years before, I hit 30 homers by the end of July.
I ended up with exactly 36. I only hit six homers in the last

two months of the year. I knew Babe smacked 17 homers in September alone. So I knew it was going to be tough. Then there was something else to worry about, being walked.

They brought up a lot of kid pitchers at the end of the season and they were apt to walk you. At least, that's what everyone believed. Who would admit to walking anybody on purpose? Especially if they were trying to break Babe's home-run record and they happened to be Jewish.

RADIO ANNOUNCER

We have had pogroms before; we have had wars before; we have had trouble with Arabs before. But never before have we had a Jewish home-run king. Greenberg has smashed 46 home runs. A home run for those who don't know is the name given to the hitting of a baseball which travels so far that the hitter can run around a big diamond before the ball is thrown back. A genuine baseball fan just can't be an anti-Semite. The name of Greenberg was shouted out in Fenway Park last week in eight different languages and in 21 different English dialects. Greenberg is another form of good-will emissary for the Jewish people.

EXT. BRIGGS STADIUM – DAY

Greenberg swings three bats, throws two of them away, and then steps up to the plate.

UMPIRE
Ball.

HANK GREENBERG
Come on, give me something to hit.

UMPIRE
Ball.

HANK GREENBERG
You can't just walk me. You've got to give me a chance.

WASHINGTON CATCHER
No one wants to go to the history books with you.

HANK GREENBERG
What do you care about it?

WASHINGTON CATCHER
What about the Babe?

HANK GREENBERG
He doesn't mind.

WASHINGTON CATCHER
How do you know?

HANK GREENBERG
Why don't you ask him yourself.

WASHINGTON CATCHER
Aw, Babe's just being nice to you.

HANK GREENBERG
Why not join the club?

WASHINGTON CATCHER
So you can get into the history books, no thanks.

HANK GREENBERG

You can tell your grandchildren about it.

WASHINGTON CATCHER

Yeah, right.

UMPIRE

Ball.

HANK GREENBERG

You're not going to be nice about it. Are you?

WASHINGTON CATCHER

We don't need some Jew breaking records.

HANK GREENBERG

At least, let me hit the ball.

UMPIRE

Ball four. Take your base.

HANK GREENBERG

Thanks for nothing.

WASHINGTON CATCHER

Now you got it, you big Jew.

HANK GREENBERG

See you soon.

WASHINGTON CATCHER

And you're not going to get anything to hit next time either.

HANK GREENBERG

Bless you.

WASHINGTON CATCHER

Yeah, right.

HANK GREENBERG VOICEOVER

I knew they couldn't walk me every time up. I mean they had to pitch to me some time. The Babe, meanwhile, said that he was on my side. Good old Babe. But not everyone felt the way the Babe felt, even if it was his record I was chasing.

EXT. PHILADELPHIA STADIUM – DAY

The Tigers are playing against the Philadelphia A's. Players are shouting from the Tiger dugout as Greenberg walks toward the plate swinging three bats.

TIGER PLAYER

Come on, Hank, park one.

TIGER PLAYER

One for the Bambino, Hank.

PHILADELPHIA CATCHER

You'll get nothing from us, big guy.

HANK GREENBERG

Well, I'll wait and see.

PHILADELPHIA CATCHER
We don't want to be part of your record, understand?

HANK GREENBERG
Well, I can hope, can't I?

PHILADELPHIA CATCHER
Hoping ain't gonna get you a fast ball down the middle.

HANK GREENBERG
I don't need it down the middle. Anything
near the strike zone would be fine.

PHILADELPHIA CATCHER
So you can beat Babe, forget it.

RADIO ANNOUNCER
Greenberg steps back into the box. Here's the
pitch, he swings, and it's a long fly ball into left field.
That's a home run and number fifty-four.

HANK GREENBERG steps on home plate and looks at the catcher.

HANK GREENBERG
You guys didn't let me down, after all.

PHILADELPHIA CATCHER
Well, it wasn't my decision to give you a meat ball.

HANK GREENBERG
It wasn't that bad of a pitch.

PHILADELPHIA CATCHER
A matzoh ball.

HANK GREENBERG
Very good, you're not Jewish, are you?

PHILADELPHIA CATCHER
No way.

HANK GREENBERG
You look Jewish.

PHILADELPHIA CATCHER
Get out of here, you son of a bitch.

HANK GREENBERG, smiling, trots to the Tiger dugout.

CHARLIE GEHRINGER
You sent that one soaring, big guy.

HANK GREENBERG
I'm ruining my swing.

CHARLIE GEHRINGER
Beat the record first and then worry about your swing.

HANK GREENBERG
Probably right.

BILLY ROGELL
Poor Bambino.

HANK GREENBERG
He probably doesn't care.

BILLY ROGELL
But his poor record, Hank.

HANK GREENBERG
He won't miss it.

BILLY ROGELL
Broken by a Jew.

HANK GREENBERG
Broken by a big Jew.

BILLY ROGELL
Oh, the good old days.

HANK GREENBERG
I don't miss them.

BILLY ROGELL
But what about the Bambino?

HANK GREENBERG
He'll get over it.

BILLY ROGELL
What about the fans?

HANK GREENBERG
They'll accept it in time.

BILLY ROGELL

How much time, Hank?

HANK GREENBERG

That's all we've got.

BILLY ROGELL

Speaking of time, we have a second game, gentlemen.

HANK GREENBERG

Time for two.

BILLY ROGELL

You got it, big guy.

HANK GREENBERG VOICEOVER

That second game was called after five innings because
of darkness. That's what happened in those days
before lights in the ball park. Anyway, it was Detroit's
142nd game – with twelve games left in the season.
Ruth had hit his fifty-fourth in his 145th game.

INT. TIGER LOCKER ROOM – DAY

The Tiger players are in the locker room dressing for the game.

HANK GREENBERG

Next summer, I'm going to hit more naturally.

CHARLIE GEHRINGER

What do you mean, Hank?

HANK GREENBERG

Manager Baker agrees with me that trying for
home runs exclusively isn't worth it.

BILLY ROGELL

It sure gets the headlines.

CHARLIE GEHRINGER

And it brings the fans to the park.

HANK GREENBERG

Yeah, but I'd be more valuable to the club
if I was loosened up more at bat.

CHARLIE GEHRINGER

Can't be too loose.

BILLY ROGELL

I like watching you hit them homers, Hank. Some
of those shots are real works of art if you ask me.
Man, some of those you really hit a ton.

CHARLIE GEHRINGER

Hank wants to be loose.

HANK GREENBERG

I'm just saying home runs aren't everything.

BILLY ROGELL

But they win ball games, I'll tell you that.

CHARLIE GEHRINGER

And the women love them.

HANK GREENBERG

I'm not saying I'm never going to hit
another homer, you understand.

CHARLIE GEHRINGER

But you want to be loose.

BILLY ROGELL

Loose as a goose.

HANK GREENBERG (smiling)

Something like that.

BILLY ROGELL

So first break the record and then you can get loose.

PETE FOX

You want to get loose, break the record.

CHARLIE GEHRINGER

Yeah, that will get you loose.

BILLY ROGELL

I wonder if the Babe was loose.

RUDY YORK

Aw, loose, just hit the darned ball.

HANK GREENBERG

But I've been overswinging.

BILLY ROGELL

Not loose enough.

PETE FOX

Just do what you've been doing, Hank.

BILLY ROGELL

But he wants to be loose.

PETE FOX

What does loose have to do with it?

HANK GREENBERG

I just said I wanted to loosen up my swing.

RUDY YORK

Aw, loosen up your head.

BILLY ROGELL

But Hank's trying to break a record.

RUDY YORK

Aw, the record.

BILLY ROGELL

The Bambino's record.

CHARLIE GEHRINGER

God bless the Bambino.

RUDY YORK

Aw, the Bambino. They make it like no one
else put on a baseball uniform.

BILLY ROGELL

But the Babe.

PETE FOX

Aw, he was just like us.

BILLY ROGELL

Except for the home runs and the money.

CHARLIE GEHRINGER

The hot dogs and the women.

BILLY ROGELL

The Bambino.

PETE FOX

What about it, Hank, are you going to break the record?

HANK GREENBERG

The record, the record, that's all I hear from everyone.

BILLY ROGELL

The Hankino.

CHARLIE GEHRINGER

Hammerin' Hank to you.

HANK GREENBERG

You know they don't want me breaking that record.

BILLY ROGELL

Why? Because you're too tall?

HANK GREENBERG

Aw, come on, you know the reason.

BILLY ROGELL

Because you weigh too much?

HANK GREENBERG

Very funny.

CHARLIE GEHRINGER

It's because he's not loose enough.

BILLY ROGELL

That's it, not loose enough.

HANK GREENBERG

They don't want some old lady keeling over because some Jewish guy broke the Babe's home run record.

BILLY ROGELL

Jewish? Are you Jewish?

HANK GREENBERG

What of it?

RUDY YORK

Who cares?

HANK GREENBERG

I wish that was true, but it isn't.

RUDY YORK

Just break the record.

CHARLIE GEHRINGER

The Bambino doesn't care. That's what it says in the papers.

BILLY ROGELL

Yeah, the Bambino doesn't care that you're Jewish.

HANK GREENBERG

He's the only one.

RUDY YORK

Stop thinking about it and go out there and hit the ball.

HANK GREENBERG

If they pitch to me.

RUDY YORK

They're going to give you something, just don't worry so much.

BILLY ROGELL

Yeah, just stay loose.

CHARLIE GEHRINGER

Loose as a goose.

HANK GREENBERG

Easy for you guys to say.

BILLY ROGELL

Yeah, Hank has to worry about the record.

CHARLIE GEHRINGER

Not just any record.

PETE FOX

Aw, homers, you can keep them.

BILLY ROGELL

But this is the home run record.

CHARLIE GEHRINGER

The Babe's record.

BILLY ROGELL

And Hank is Jewish.

CHARLIE GEHRINGER

What did you say?

BILLY ROGELL

Jewish.

HARRY EISENSTAT

With the horns and the eating of children?

BILLY ROGELL

Yes, Jewish.

HANK GREENBERG
I plead guilty as charged.

BILLY ROGELL
He pleads guilty.

PETE FOX
Aw, a Jew.

BILLY ROGELL
Guilty as charged.

CHARLIE GEHRINGER
A Jew?

BILLY ROGELL
Guilty as charged.

HANK GREENBERG
Trying to beat the Bambino.

BILLY ROGELL
The Bambino?

CHARLIE GEHRINGER
Heresy.

PETE FOX
Aw, the Bambino.

BILLY ROGELL
Do you love your country?

HANK GREENBERG

You mean because a Jew is trying to break the Bambino's record?

BILLY ROGELL

You got it.

HANK GREENBERG

Guilty as charged, but I love my country.

CHARLIE GEHRINGER

But the Bambino is America.

BILLY ROGELL

Hot dogs and baseball.

HANK GREENBERG

No, America is for everybody.

BILLY ROGELL

Communist.

HANK GREENBERG

No, everybody has a chance in America.

HARRY EISENSTAT

Even a Jew?

HANK GREENBERG

Even a Jew.

CHARLIE GEHRINGER

Heresy.

BILLY ROGELL

Burn him at the stake.

HANK GREENBERG

Hey, I'm just trying to break a record.

BILLY ROGELL

The Bambino's record.

RUDY YORK

Aw, the Bambino.

BILLY ROGELL

Hot dogs and baseball.

CHARLIE GEHRINGER

The American pastime.

HANK GREENBERG

It's just a record.

BILLY ROGELL

The Babe's record.

RUDY YORK

Aw, come on, the Babe can't have every record.

BILLY ROGELL

But it's the home run record.

RUDY YORK

Yeah, yeah, home runs.

Adam Pfeffer

BILLY ROGELL
But a Jew.

CHARLIE GEHRINGER
What about God?

HANK GREENBERG
Was He pitching?

HARRY EISENSTAT
God.

HANK GREENBERG
I need all the help I can get.

BILLY ROGELL
God, Hank.

HANK GREENBERG
Something we can agree on.

BILLY ROGELL
But it's the Babe's record.

HANK GREENBERG
And meant to be broken.

CHARLIE GEHRINGER
You got it, Hank.

RUDY YORK
Go out there and break it.

PETE FOX
Break it.

BILLY ROGELL
Break it.

HANK GREENBERG
That's what I intend to do.

HANK GREENBERG VOICEOVER
But it wasn't so easy breaking that record. Maybe the guys were
right. The record had something to do with God, country, hot
dogs and baseball. Nobody wanted some Jew to come along and
take it from the Babe. But I didn't care. Records were meant
to be broken, and I was aiming to break that record if I could.

EXT. BRIGGS STADIUM, DETROIT – DAY 1938

The Detroit Tigers are playing the Cleveland Indians with Hank
Greenberg at the plate.

HANK GREENBERG
Come on, Earl, give me something I can hit.

INDIAN CATCHER
You know Earl?

HANK GREENBERG
We played together.

INDIAN CATCHER

Well, that's not going to do you any good today.

HANK GREENBERG

You've decided not to pitch to me?

INDIAN CATCHER

We'll pitch to you, but you're not going to break the record today.

HANK GREENBERG

The record, the record, that's all I hear about.

INDIAN CATCHER

It's the Babe's record.

HANK GREENBERG

But it's only a record.

INDIAN CATCHER

To a Jew.

HANK GREENBERG

Someone has to break it.

INDIAN CATCHER

Not a Jew.

HANK GREENBERG

We're no different than anyone else.

INDIAN CATCHER

Yeah, right.

HANK GREENBERG
Just pitch the ball.

UMPIRE
Ball.

HANK GREENBERG
Come on, Earl, give me a chance to hit the ball.

INDIAN CATCHER
You're going down, Jew.

UMPIRE
Strike.

INDIAN CATCHER
What about that one, Jew, why don't you swing?

HANK GREENBERG
I'll swing when I'm ready. You just make sure
he's aiming for the strike zone.

HANK GREENBERG swings at the next pitch and there is a loud
noise as the bat connects with the ball.

INDIAN CATCHER
Son of a bitch.

HANK GREENBERG
Thanks for everything.

INDIAN CATCHER
You big Jew.

Adam Pfeffer

RADIO ANNOUNCER

There's a long home run off the bat of Hammerin' Hank Greenberg, ladies and gentlemen. That's number fifty-five for the season and only five away from the record by Babe Ruth.

HANK GREENBERG runs around the bases and trots to the dugout.

BILLY ROGELL

You got it, Hank. Take that, Bambino.

CHARLIE GEHRINGER

Way to go, Hank, you're almost there.

HANK GREENBERG

Good old Earl Whitehill. He served me a nice meat ball.

BILLY ROGELL

You need all the meat balls you can get.

PETE FOX

Aw, meat balls.

HANK GREENBERG

If the Babe only knew.

BILLY ROGELL

If the Babe only knew you knew Earl.

HANK GREENBERG

I'm going to send him a Christmas card.

CHARLIE GEHRINGER
Good Yontif.

HANK GREENBERG
Or Merry Christmas.

BILLY ROGELL
Whatever.

HANK GREENBERG
Earl really deserves a card.

PETE FOX
Aw, just break the record.

HANK GREENBERG
You've got it, Pete, the record.

RADIO ANNOUNCER
Here comes Hammerin' Hank Greenberg to the plate, ladies and gentlemen. The slugging first baseman already has hit one home run today to bring his season total to fifty-five.

HANK GREENBERG
So we meet again.

INDIAN CATCHER
We stopped serving meat balls, Jew.

HANK GREENBERG
That's fine with me as long as you throw something.

INDIAN CATCHER

You're not going to break the record, anyway.

HANK GREENBERG

Yeah, and why not?

INDIAN CATCHER

Because you're a Jew, and no Jew is going to break the record.

HANK GREENBERG

You don't believe in God?

INDIAN CATCHER

God doesn't care about some Jew breaking the record.

HANK GREENBERG

That's not what Moses said.

INDIAN CATCHER

You can keep your Moses and everything
else. No Jew is breaking the record.

RADIO ANNOUNCER

Here's the pitch from Earl Whitehill and it's a long wallop
to left field. That ball is gone for Greenberg's fifty-sixth
homer of the season, and only four away from the record.

EXT. BRIGGS STADIUM – DAY 1938

Greenberg trots around the bases as the fans cheer.

HANK GREENBERG

Thanks again.

INDIAN CATCHER

You big Jew.

Hank Greenberg steps on home plate and then trots to the Tiger dugout.

RADIO ANNOUNCER

Well, one record was broken today, ladies and gentlemen. Greenberg set the mark for hitting two homers in one game most often during a single season. He has done it ten times so far in 1938.

DEL BAKER

Nice piece of hitting, Hank.

HANK GREENBERG

Thanks, skip.

BILLY ROGELL

You're almost there, Hank.

CHARLIE GEHRINGER

The Bambino's rooting for you.

HANK GREENBERG

I sure hope so, Charlie.

BILLY ROGELL

At least they're pitching to you.

HANK GREENBERG

Yeah, good old Earl.

HANK GREENBERG VOICEOVER

All I heard about was the record. I lived it, breathed it, and kept thinking about it. What was so important about the record, anyway? I really didn't know except it was the Babe's record and it was the home-run record, the most glamorous in baseball. Nobody really wanted me to break it. It belonged to the Bambino, case closed. But I didn't care. I would keep swinging for the fences because I was so close to breaking that darned record. Even if the only ones who wanted me to break it were Jewish. I was finding that out the hard way. No more pitches in the strike zone, no more home runs, they figured. If anyone complained, they just said the pitchers were tired and wild at the end of the season and that everybody had a few more walks near the end of the schedule. I didn't want to hear it, didn't believe it. This was America, baseball and the land of the free. What was so important about that darned record, anyway?

RADIO ANNOUNCER

Here's Hank Greenberg walking up to the plate, ladies and gentlemen. Hammerin' Hank hit two homers yesterday and now has fifty-six for the season. The record is, of course, held by Babe Ruth, who had 60.

INDIAN CATCHER

You'll get nothing today.

HANK GREENBERG

Just keep your glove in the strike zone.

INDIAN CATCHER

You saying we're walking you on purpose?

HANK GREENBERG

I wouldn't think of saying that.

INDIAN CATCHER

Good, because this is supposed to be a clean game.

HANK GREENBERG

Just remember that.

INDIAN CATCHER

You'll get your chance to swing that bat.

HANK GREENBERG

That's all I'm asking.

INDIAN CATCHER

And that's what you'll get.

UMPIRE

Ball.

HANK GREENBERG

That's what I thought.

INDIAN CATCHER

You thought right.

UMPIRE

Ball Two.

HANK GREENBERG

Aw, give me a chance.

INDIAN CATCHER
We already gave you a chance.

HANK GREENBERG
The darned record.

INDIAN CATCHER
It's the Babe's record.

HANK GREENBERG
You don't have to tell me.

UMPIRE
Ball Three.

HANK GREENBERG
Well, I guess I won't be breaking it today.

INDIAN CATCHER
You got that right.

UMPIRE
Sttttttrike.

INDIAN CATCHER
That was your pitch.

HANK GREENBERG
With a three and oh count, I'm taking all the way.

INDIAN CATCHER
I thought you were a Jew.

HANK GREENBERG

Why, because I'm taking?

INDIAN CATCHER

At least you're not greedy.

HANK GREENBERG

Yeah, why not give me another?

INDIAN CATCHER

Jew.

UMPIRE

Ball Four, take your base.

HANK GREENBERG

Well, that was interesting.

INDIAN CATCHER

That's for the Babe.

HANK GREENBERG

Well, I'm sure he's happy.

INDIAN CATCHER

As long as you're not.

HANK GREENBERG

Good day, sir.

INDIAN CATCHER

Come back and you'll get the same.

HANK GREENBERG VOICEOVER

And they meant it, too. I just kept telling myself that walks are bound to happen, especially at the end of the season, but everybody knew something was going on. I mean we weren't in the pennant race, but still there were some good pitchers left on every roster at the end of the season. Baseball people were saying the pitchers were tired, but nobody really believed it. I was going after that damned record. Everybody thought a greedy Jew was going after a record, the Babe's record. I knew differently. I wanted that record just because it was within reach. No other reason. All those hypocrites would have done exactly the same thing.

RADIO ANNOUNCER

Hammerin' Hank Greenberg has walked for the second time today, his home run total remaining at 56. Hank is still three games ahead of Ruth's pace. He has 56 homers in 145 games if he doesn't hit one today. The Babe had 56 in 148 games.

EXT. BRIGGS STADIUM, DETROIT – DAY 1938

The Detroit Tigers are playing the St. Louis Browns in Detroit.

TIGER PLAYER
Come on, Hank, hit it out.

TIGER PLAYER
One at a time, Hank.

Hank Greenberg swings three bats as he walks towards home plate.

HANK GREENBERG

Hello, gentlemen.

He throws two bats away and steps up to the plate.

UMPIRE

Ball one.

HANK GREENBERG

I'm just going to wait for my pitch.

BROWNS CATCHER

No meat balls today.

HANK GREENBERG

Aw, I don't need a meat ball.

UMPIRE

Strike.

HANK GREENBERG

He's got to give me something.

BROWNS CATCHER

Not today.

Hank Greenberg uncoils his arms and swings at the next pitch. There's a bang and the ball sails towards the outfield fence. Hank Greenberg rounds first base and heads to second base. The fans are screaming as Greenberg heads to third.

RADIO ANNOUNCER

Here's Greenberg rounding third and heading for home. Here

comes the throw and Greenberg slides into the plate. He's safe for an inside-the-park homer and his fifty-seventh of the year.

BROWNS PLAYER (arguing)
You've got to be kidding, he was out.

BROWNS CATCHER
What kind of call was that? He was out by a mile.

Hank Greenberg trots to the Tiger dugout.

BILLY ROGELL
That's fifty-seven, Hank.

HANK GREENBERG
Too close for my taste.

CHARLIE GEHRINGER
Nice hustling, Hank.

HANK GREENBERG
No one was going to stop me when I reached third.

BILLY ROGELL
Oh, Hank, the Babe called. He said you were out.

HANK GREENBERG
Tell the Babe he might be right.

DEL BAKER
Whew, what a close one.

HANK GREENBERG VOICEOVER

Forty years later, I got a letter from Sam Harshaney, who was a reserve catcher with the Browns. The letter said: "Dear Hank: My boys have now grown and have gone off to college. I have been telling them for years that you never hit that home run and that you were out at the plate. Could you get a picture showing that particular incident?"

I wrote back and said, "I'm sorry, I have no picture, but you are absolutely right. I was out by a mile and had no business being called safe. So you can tell your boys that their dad stopped Hank Greenberg from getting home run number 57."

RADIO ANNOUNCER

Here's the pitch from Bill Cox. Greenberg swings and it's way back there. That's Greenberg's fifty-eighth homer of the season. Holy Cow!

Greenberg trots around the bases as the fans cheer.

BILLY ROGELL (from the bench)
Some shot, Hank.

CHARLIE GEHRINGER
Just a few more, Hank.

Greenberg runs to the dugout, shaking hands.

HANK GREENBERG
Thanks, guys.

BILLY ROGELL
Hey, it's the Babe's record, Hank, just remember that.

HANK GREENBERG (smiling)

I will until I break it.

RADIO ANNOUNCER

Well, Greenberg has hit 58 homers in 149 games and has
five games left to break the record. Ruth didn't hit his
fifty-eighth until the 152nd game of the 1927 season.

HANK GREENBERG VOICEOVER

When I crossed the plate for my fifty-eighth home run, I thought
I had a chance to do it. Break the precious record. We had two
games in Detroit and three in Cleveland. I thought I would get
three more easily. I figured I would get about twenty at-bats, and
even if the pitchers were extra careful, I'd still get about twenty-
five good pitches to swing at. At least, that's how I figured it.

INT. DETROIT TIGER LOCKER ROOM – DAY 1938

HANK GREENBERG (reading)

"There is no shuffle of marching feet, no roar of armored
tanks down well-paved streets. No frightening banners
of war and all its ghastly consequences. But in Detroit
at least the question still is, 'Can he make it?'"

BILLY ROGELL

They make it as if you're fighting Hitler, Hank.

HANK GREENBERG

In some way, I guess I am. You see, some are saying my people
are inferior and different from others. I have to show that Hitler

and the Nazis are as wrong as could be and the things they are saying are nonsense. I am fighting Hitler in my own way.

CHARLIE GEHRINGER (reading)

Listen to this, Hank. "The closer Greenberg gets to the record, the more eager Babe Ruth is to admit the chances of it being broken. 'He should break it – in that park,' was Babe's view of the situation yesterday, a statement which would have ended better if Babe had omitted any reference to the Detroit ballpark."

BILLY ROGELL

I guess there's nothing there about the
short porch at Yankee Stadium.

CHARLIE GEHRINGER

Yeah, that the Babe fails to mention.

HANK GREENBERG

Well, at least we know now how the Babe feels. If I break
the record, it's because it's an easy ball park to hit in.

BILLY ROGELL

What bunk.

CHARLIE GEHRINGER

There's always some excuse.

HANK GREENBERG

There always will be some excuse as long as I'm Jewish.

BILLY ROGELL

It really shouldn't matter.

HANK GREENBERG

Go tell the Nazis and everyone else. A lot of people still think we have horns in our head.

BILLY ROGELL

It's all out of ignorance.

HANK GREENBERG

Yeah, I guess.

CHARLIE GEHRINGER

We don't hate you, Hank.

HANK GREENBERG

Thanks a lot. You're good teammates.

BILLY ROGELL

Go out there and break the record, Hank. It would be the best thing that ever happened to this hateful world.

HANK GREENBERG

I'm going to try, you can bet on that.

HANK GREENBERG VOICEOVER

The St. Louis Browns were in Detroit for two games. They weren't very good but they decided to pitch Bobo Newsom, their best pitcher. He was going for his twentieth win of the season. I had a hard time hitting Newsom. That day I could only manage a double. The next day the last-place Browns pitched Howard Mills, a lefty. They said he was nervous and wild.

EXT. BRIGGS STADIUM, DETROIT – DAY 1938

Greenberg walks up to the plate holding a bat and a grin.

HANK GREENBERG

Hello, gentlemen.

BROWNS CATCHER

Mills is all over the place today so don't expect anything today.

HANK GREENBERG

I'll take whatever he gives me.

UMPIRE

Ball one.

HANK GREENBERG

He's not giving me a lot.

BROWNS CATCHER

He's nervous and this crowd booing is
making him even more nervous.

HANK GREENBERG

I'll smile.

UMPIRE

Ball two.

HANK GREENBERG

I think he's looking better.

Adam Pfeffer

BROWNS CATCHER

That's what you say.

The next pitch Greenberg swings and the ball darts high and far into left field.

RADIO ANNOUNCER

That's long and far. Man, that hits the roof
in left field, but it's a foul ball.

BROWNS CATCHER

Just missed, Jew.

HANK GREENBERG

That's the first time I ever hit that roof. Figures it was foul.

UMPIRE

Ball.

HANK GREENBERG

Damn, I think I made Mills nervous again.

BROWNS CATCHER

You sure did.

HANK GREENBERG

I'll smile again.

UMPIRE

Ball four, take your base.

HANK GREENBERG VOICEOVER

Well, that would be the closest I came to a home run that day.

Howard Mills remained nervous and wild the entire game. He ended up walking me twice I would have walked a third time, but I decided to swing at anything that was close in any way. I ended up striking out twice and hitting a pop fly. We won the game, 12 to nothing, with eleven hits, but none of them were by me. When I came up, Howard Mills was nervous and wild. The booing of the fans only made him more nervous and wild. At least that's what they told me. Anyway, the Babe was safe for another day.

Hank Greenberg walks up to the plate against the St. Louis Browns.

HANK GREENBERG
Hello, gentlemen.

BROWNS CATCHER
Hello yourself.

UMPIRE
Ball one.

BROWNS CATCHER
Time out.

The Browns catcher trots out to the Browns pitcher.

BROWNS CATCHER
What are you doing? I asked for a fast ball.

BROWNS PITCHER
He's not going to break a record with my name in the paper.

BROWNS CATCHER

You're up here to pitch. You're not up here
to put somebody on base purposely.

BROWNS PITCHER

Aw, come on, get back behind the plate.

BROWNS CATCHER

Try not to hit him.

HANK GREENBERG VOICEOVER

Sure, there was added pressure being Jewish. How the hell
could you get up to home plate every day and have some son
of a bitch call you a Jew bastard and a kike and a sheenie and
get on your ass without feeling the pressure. If the ballplayers
weren't doing it, the fans were. I used to get frustrated as hell.
Sometimes I wanted to go up in the stands and beat the shit
out of them. Then there was the record. I was representing
a couple of million Jews among a hundred million gentiles,
and I was always in the spotlight. I wanted to show them
that a Jewish person could play ball. I wanted to show the
whole world of hate and meanness that a Jewish person could
do anything he wanted to do and nobody, not the Nazis or
anybody else, could stop him. Then there were the walks.
They kept walking me and I kept trying to break the record.

EXT. BRIGGS STADIUM, DETROIT – DAY 1938

Greenberg goes into the Tiger dugout.

BILLY ROGELL

They're not giving you anything to hit, Hank.

HANK GREENBERG

Yeah, Babe is still safe.

BILLY ROGELL

They won't let you break it, I guess.

HANK GREENBERG

I'm not really surprised.

BILLY ROGELL

They don't want you to beat the Babe's record.

HANK GREENBERG

Because I'm Jewish?

BILLY ROGELL

Not just because you're Jewish, but that has a lot to do with it.

HANK GREENBERG

Oh, well, it's only a record.

BILLY ROGELL

You know the guys on the club are pulling like hell for you.

HANK GREENBERG

There's nothing I wouldn't do for my teammates.

BILLY ROGELL

We all have our fingers crossed for you, Hank.

HANK GREENBERG

I love you guys.

BILLY ROGELL

Hit a home run, Hank, break the damned record.

HANK GREENBERG

I'm going to try.

BILLY ROGELL

That's what any one of us would say, Hank.

HANK GREENBERG

Well, I'm just like you guys.

BILLY ROGELL

I never believed that before, but you are, Hank.

HANK GREENBERG

That's what people don't understand.

BILLY ROGELL

You're one of us, Hank.

HANK GREENBERG

That's great, Billy. I'm happy you said that.

HANK GREENBERG VOICEOVER

There were now three games left in the season, all with the Indians in Cleveland. There was talk that Cleveland was going to move the fences back to prevent me from breaking the record, but I guess that was only the rumor. I still needed two home runs to tie the record and three to break it. I really wanted to break it, but I would have to wait to see if they pitched to me. It rained on Friday so they scheduled a doubleheader for Sunday, October 2. I would still have a few chances to break the damned record.

EXT. LEAGUE PARK, CLEVELAND – DAY 1938

Greenberg walks up to the plate swinging three bats. He throws two of them down and steps into the batter's box.

HANK GREENBERG
Hello, gentlemen.

INDIAN CATCHER
Just get up there.

UMPIRE
Stttrike one.

HANK GREENBERG
Just give me something I can handle.

INDIAN CATCHER
You won't get it from Denny, not today.

RADIO ANNOUNCER
Denny Galehouse is pitching the greatest game of his life today as Hank Greenberg is stuck on fifty-eight home runs. Here's the pitch to Greenberg and it's a grounder to second. It looks as if Hammerin' Hank won't be breaking the record today, ladies and gentlemen. Greenberg is thrown out at first and the Indians lead, five to nothing. Greenberg is apparently mighty mad. He is kicking bats off the rack in front of the Tiger dugout. There's a lot of pressure on Hank as he goes for the record.

EXT. TIGER DUGOUT – DAY 1938

Hank Greenberg is standing by the Tiger dugout, pulling the bats off the bat rack.

HANK GREENBERG (throwing the bats in front of the dugout)
The damned morons. They just won't give me anything to hit.

BILLY ROGELL (in the dugout)
Aw, Hank, don't let them know they're getting to you.

ELDEN AUKER
Let him let off some steam, the record's killing him.

RUDY YORK
Aw, forget the record, Hank, it's not that important.

BILLY ROGELL
It is to him.

HANK GREENBERG (stepping into the dugout)
Dirty, rotten criminals.

CHARLIE GEHRINGER
You still have tomorrow, Hank.

JO-JO WHITE
Yeah, they're bound to let you have something tomorrow.

HANK GREENBERG
Tomorrow and tomorrow. I live for today.

CHARLIE GEHRINGER

Come on, Hank, the guy pitched a great game.

HANK GREENBERG

They all do against me.

BILLY ROGELL

You'll get your chance.

HANK GREENBERG

Yeah, tomorrow. And what do they have in store for tomorrow?

JO-JO WHITE

Nothing you won't be able to handle.

PETE FOX

Aw, the record.

BILLY ROGELL

You'll have a chance in the doubleheader.

RUDY YORK

Yeah, you'll get your chance.

HANK GREENBERG

Dirty, rotten criminals.

HANK GREENBERG VOICEOVER

Denny Galehouse pitched the game of his life. He shut us out and I went oh for four. It seemed everything was against me and then I heard the news of what they had planned for me on the last day of the season. They moved the doubleheader from League Park to the much larger Municipal Stadium. They said it was to capitalize on my chasing the home run record and that they would get more fans into the ballpark. The Indians said they switched most Sunday and holiday games to Municipal Stadium. Old League Park was a tough enough park for a right-handed hitter to hit a home run in – it was 374 feet down the left-field line – but Municipal Stadium was almost impossible.

INT. TIGER LOCKER ROOM – DAY 1938

HANK GREENBERG

Dirty scoundrels. They're not even going to give me a fair shot.

DEL BAKER

Sorry, Hank, but we have to play by their rules.

HANK GREENBERG

You know who's pitching in the first game?

JO-JO WHITE

Their best, Hank.

HANK GREENBERG

You got it. Rapid Robert himself, Bob Feller.

CHARLIE GEHRINGER

He's got some heater.

BILLY ROGELL

You just get scared he's going to uncork one.

HANK GREENBERG

You can't dig in against Rapid Robert.

RUDY YORK

But if you connect, it's going to go a long way.

HANK GREENBERG

If you connect.

RADIO ANNOUNCER

Welcome to the first game of today's doubleheader, the last games of the season. Rapid Robert, Bob Feller, will be going up against left-hander Harry Eisenstat. The real drama of today's twin bill is Hammerin' Hank Greenberg's quest for the Major League home run record held by Babe Ruth. Greenberg has 58, the Babe finished with 60. Can he do it? It's going to be tough today because the game is being played in Municipal Stadium, a larger park the Indians use for Sundays and holidays. Bob Feller said before the game, he was going "to make Greenberg earn any home runs he hits off me."

EXT. CLEVELAND'S MUNICIPAL STADIUM – DAY 1938

HANK GREENBERG walks up to the plate.

HANK GREENBERG

Fine day for a ball game.

INDIANS CATCHER

Don't expect any mercy.

HANK GREENBERG

I'm just here to give it my best shot.

INDIANS CATCHER

Feller says he has no pity for you.

HANK GREENBERG

And I thought he was going to lay one right in there for me.

INDIANS CATCHER

Not today, you big Jew.

RADIO ANNOUNCER

Here's the pitch from Feller and it's a strike. Man, is he throwing hard out there. Well, there's no tomorrow and here's the pitch. It's smacked by Greenberg into left center. That ball is way back there. Is it going to go? No, off the wall for a double. Greenberg was so close to getting his fifty-ninth, but it wasn't to be. He's standing there on second base shaking his head. Whew, that was close.

HANK GREENBERG VOICEOVER

The ball I hit against Feller wasn't far enough. But I still had a few more chances. He was throwing hard, but I felt pretty good on that last day of the season.

RADIO ANNOUNCER

Here's Hammerin' Hank Greenberg once again, ladies and gentlemen. Greenberg is stuck on fifty-eight homers with only a few at bats left in today's first game of a scheduled doubleheader. He is trying to tie Babe Ruth's record of 60.

The Tiger players are shouting from the dugout.

JO-JO WHITE

Come on, Hank, hit it out of here.

CHARLIE GEHRINGER

Just wait for your pitch, big guy.

RADIO ANNOUNCER

Here's the pitch from Feller and Greenberg smacks it to deep centerfield. That ball is way back there. Here comes Roy Weatherly, the centerfielder, who makes a running one-handed stab to prevent Greenberg from hitting it out of here. Oh my, what a shot by Greenberg and what a play by Weatherly. Greenberg is shaking his head as he goes back to the Tiger dugout. The Babe's record is still safe, ladies and gentlemen.

CHARLIE GEHRINGER

That was a close one, Hank

BILLY ROGELL

The guy made a nice play.

PETE FOX

Can't do anything about that.

HANK GREENBERG

Well, that just about does it, gentlemen.

JO-JO WHITE

You still have a few more chances, Hank.

HANK GREENBERG

Yeah, a few more chances.

RADIO ANNOUNCER

Here comes Hammerin' Hank Greenberg once again, ladies and gentlemen. Hank has hit a double today off Bob Feller and a long fly ball that was caught in deep centerfield. Here's the pitch for ball one. Greenberg has also struck out twice today against the fireballer Rapid Robert. Here's the next pitch and it's a ball. Well, Feller seems as if he wants nothing to do with Hank Greenberg, who is chasing Babe Ruth's vaunted home run record here on the last day of the baseball season. The next pitch by Feller is in there for a strike. The count is now two and one to Greenberg.

HANK GREENBERG

You guys are making it tough for me.

INDIANS CATCHER

You better concentrate.

HANK GREENBERG

Feller's had it with me.

UMPIRE

Ball three.

HANK GREENBERG

Nothing down the middle.

INDIANS CATCHER

Aw, you had your chance today.

UMPIRE

Ball four, take your base.

HANK GREENBERG

Give Bob my regards.

INDIANS CATCHER
There goes the record.

HANK GREENBERG
Only a record, my friend.

HANK GREENBERG VOICEOVER
We beat Bob Feller that day in the first game of the doubleheader, four to one, but I didn't hit anything out for a home run. Harry Eisenstat, a small left-hander from Brooklyn, who I hung around with considering we both were Jewish, got the win. Birdie Tebbetts, the Detroit catcher, told us Feller was throwing about 105 miles an hour, with a curve at about 95 miles an hour. He struck out eighteen of us that day, a record at the time. Eisenstat, meanwhile, was throwing about 81 miles an hour, according to Birdie, struck out three guys and won the game. I had one game left to beat the record. Some said it was still possible since I had hit two homers in eleven different games that season. But I knew it would be pretty hard to do it now.

RADIO ANNOUNCER
Welcome to the last game of the season, ladies and gentlemen, with the Cleveland Indians playing the Detroit Tigers at Municipal Stadium in Cleveland, Ohio. The game is notable in that it is Hank Greenberg's last chance to break Babe Ruth's home run record of 60. Greenberg has 58 homers, but should get about four at bats.

HARRY EISENSTAT
You still have a shot at it, Hank.

HANK GREENBERG
I need a little luck.

HARRY EISENSTAT
You don't need luck, you've got something better, talent.

HANK GREENBERG
It's always nice to have some luck.

HARRY EISENSTAT
Good luck, Hank.

HANK GREENBERG
Thanks, Harry.

HANK GREENBERG VOICEOVER
The starting pitcher for the Indians was Johnny Humphries, a rookie pitcher who was almost as fast as Feller. He looked even faster because the shadows started to creep across the field in the second game of the doubleheader. In those days there were no lights and therefore, it was pretty hard to hit as it got darker and darker. This was my last shot to tie or beat the record and I decided I would go out there and do my best.

RADIO ANNOUNCER
Here's Hank Greenberg stepping up to the plate. Humphries delivers and Greenberg lines a single to left field. A nice hit by Hammerin' Hank but not the home run he needs for the record.

EXT. TIGER DUGOUT AT MUNICIPAL STADIUM, CLEVELAND – DAY 1938

BILLY ROGELL
It's getting darker out there.

CHARLIE GEHRINGER
There's not much time left.

HANK GREENBERG

Well, I gave it a good shot.

JO-JO WHITE

You still have a few more at bats.

HANK GREENBERG

Yeah, but soon it's going to be too dark to see.

CHARLIE GEHRINGER

And Humphries isn't getting any slower.

HANK GREENBERG

Aw, it's the Babe's record, anyway.

BILLY ROGELL

If you say so, Hank.

HANK GREENBERG

I'm going to give it one more shot.

RADIO ANNOUNCER

Here's Hank Greenberg once again, ladies and gentlemen. He only has a few more chances to tie or break Babe Ruth's home run record. He needs two homers to tie and three to break it. Here's the pitch from Humphries and Greenberg takes a mighty cut. He means business, ladies and gentlemen, no doubt about it. Humphries delivers and (crack of the bat) there's a shot by Greenberg back to the wall. That's long and far but not enough. The ball crashes into the wall, about 420 feet away. Greenberg, however, is held to a single. My, oh my, that was almost gone, ladies and gentlemen.

Adam Pfeffer

EXT. DETROIT DUGOUT – DAY 1938

HANK GREENBERG
That was pretty close.

HARRY EISENSTAT
Just a few more inches, Hank.

HANK GREENBERG
Damn, it's getting hard to see the ball.

JO-JO WHITE
Don't give up yet, big guy.

HANK GREENBERG
As long as they keep pitching, I'll keep hitting.

CHARLIE GEHRINGER
That's the way to go.

RADIO ANNOUNCER
Hammerin' Hank Greenberg comes to the plate. Hank is two for
two today with two singles, but he's looking to hit home runs.
He's right now two short of the Babe's all-time record. Here's
the pitch by Humphries and it's in there for a strike. Greenberg
is stuck on fifty-eight homers for the season. The pitch from
Humphries and Greenberg lines it into left field for a single. I don't
know how many more plate appearances he's going to have, ladies
and gentlemen. Babe Ruth's record seems pretty safe so far today.

EXT. MUNICIPAL STADIUM, CLEVELAND – DAY 1938

HANK GREENBERG

Can't get anything to drive up into the air.

JO-JO WHITE

It's tough today, Hank, those shadows
creeping in are pretty tough.

CHARLIE GEHRINGER

Too bad we can't play this one tomorrow.

HANK GREENBERG

Aw, it would be something else tomorrow.

HARRY EISENSTAT

Well, you still have at least two more at bats, Hank.

HANK GREENBERG

I won't be able to see the ball, anyway.

RADIO ANNOUNCER

Hank Greenberg steps up to the plate, ladies and gentlemen.
Hammerin' Hank is three for three today with three singles,
but no home runs. Homers are what he's looking for since
he's only two away from tying the all-time record. Here's
the pitch and it's upstairs for ball one. Hank leads the
league in walks as he tries to capture Babe Ruth's home
run record. Here's the pitch, outside, for ball two.

HANK GREENBERG

Aw, put it in there. Give me a chance.

UMPIRE

Ball three.

INDIANS CATCHER

No record for you.

HANK GREENBERG

I already got the hint.

UMPIRE

Strike one. Three and one.

HANK GREENBERG

Okay, let me have one last shot.

UMPIRE

Ball four, take your base.

HANK GREENBERG

They're all criminals.

INDIANS CATCHER

Aw, tell it to the judge.

RADIO ANNOUNCER

Greenberg is walked for the 119th time this year, ladies and gentlemen, tied with Jimmie Foxx for the Major League lead. He trots down to first base with little hope of breaking Babe Ruth's mighty record of 60 home runs. He gave it a good shot, though, and still might get another at bat in this ballgame.

HANK GREENBERG VOICEOVER

It kept getting darker and darker. Remember, there were

no lights in those days. By the seventh inning, I knew the chase was over. The umpire was George Moriarty, my friend, but even he couldn't keep that game going.

UMPIRE

I'm sorry, Hank, but this is as far as I can go.

HANK GREENBERG

That's all right, George, this is as far as I can go, too.

HANK GREENBERG VOICEOVER

They called that game after seven innings and the record was safe for another year. Of course, I was disappointed, but I never really thought of myself as a home run hitter like the Babe. My goal in baseball was always RBIs, to break Gehrig's record of 184 RBIs. I would have loved to do that. I came awfully close, within one RBI, but never did it. I always felt that Walter Briggs, the new owner of the Tigers, was pulling for me not to break the record because it would mean paying me an additional five to ten thousand dollars. Some said I didn't get the record because I was Jewish. To that accusation, I always say, pure baloney.

EXT. BRIGGS STADIUM, DETROIT – DAY 1939

Hank Greenberg hits a long home run to left field and trots around the bases.

BIRDIE TEBBETTS

Nice shot, Hank.

BILLY ROGELL
Way to go, big guy.

HANK GREENBERG (getting to the dugout)
Thanks, guys.

HANK GREENBERG VOICEOVER
I hit only 33 homers in 1939, second in the league to Jimmie Foxx, who hit 35. The Tigers, however, finished in fifth place in the American League. While I didn't have a sensational year, I did lead the team in batting with a .312 average and knocked in 112 runs, which was good for fourth in the American League. So it wasn't a disaster of a season as far as I was concerned. 1940, however, started off with a bang. Jack Zeller, the Tiger general manager, wanted to see me.

JACK ZELLER
Hello, Hank, I hope you're having a good offseason.

HANK GREENBERG
Everything's fine, what did you want to see me about?

JACK ZELLER
We have a problem, Hank. A big problem. It concerns Rudy York. It seems he can't cut it in the outfield nor behind the plate. You know we need his bat in the lineup, Hank.

HANK GREENBERG
How can I help?

JACK ZELLER
Well, Hank, we believe Rudy's natural position is first base.

HANK GREENBERG

First base?

JACK ZELLER

Yes, Hank, I know you've been there for years.
But we were thinking that maybe it wouldn't
be so bad to move you to the outfield.

HANK GREENBERG

Outfield? But I've never played any position other than first
base. I've never worn a finger mitt in a Major League game.

JACK ZELLER

Well, you know, you didn't have the year
we expected from you, Hank.

HANK GREENBERG

I led the team in hitting.

JACK ZELLER

But homeruns were down.

HANK GREENBERG

I hit 58 in '38, naturally, I had fewer last year.

JACK ZELLER

Well, Hank, we're going to cut your salary $5,000.
That's if you insist on staying at first base.

HANK GREENBERG

You looking to trade me?

Adam Pfeffer

JACK ZELLER
You know I can't tell you that.

HANK GREENBERG
You think my salary's too high or that Rudy can replace me?

JACK ZELLER
We just want you to move to left field.

HANK GREENBERG
Hmmm, all right, Mr. Zeller, I'll go to left field, but you pay me the same amount of money I received last year -- $40,000. Now I'll go down to spring training and put on a finger mitt and work out in left field and work real hard to learn the position. If, at the end of spring training, the organization is satisfied and think I can do the job in left field, then you would give me a bonus of $10,000.

JACK ZELLER
Aw, Hank, be reasonable.

HANK GREENBERG
On the other hand, if you thought I couldn't play left, then I would go back to first and it would be up to you what you wanted to do. Either you keep York or get rid of me.

JACK ZELLER
It's really not too bad.

HANK GREENBERG
Will you agree?

JACK ZELLER
I'll agree that if you are in the lineup in left field on opening day, I'll give you the ten-thousand dollar bonus.

HANK GREENBERG

Great, Mr. Zeller.

JACK ZELLER

But you work hard, Hank, remember that. You
learn the position and do a good job for us.

HANK GREENBERG

I'll do that, Mr. Zeller, I'll do that.

RADIO ANNOUNCER

Welcome to opening day, ladies and gentlemen.
Starting in left field for the Tigers will be Hank
Greenberg, the all-star first baseman.

HANK GREENBERG VOICEOVER

The first thing I did on opening day was go to the club office
and pick up my $10,000 bonus that was agreed upon. They
gave it to me and everything was fine. But a week or so after
the season opened we were in Cleveland in League Park.

EXT. LEAGUE PARK IN CLEVELAND – DAY 1940

Hank Greenberg is in left field for the Tigers. A ball is hit to the
shallow left field line.

RADIO ANNOUNCER

There's a ball hit to the left-field line. Higgins and Bartell are
going for it. Greenberg has pulled up in left field and none
of them are going to catch it. It drops for a hit and two runs

are in. Now Pete Fox is going out to left field, presumably to replace Greenberg. Oh my, ladies and gentlemen.

Pete Fox runs out to left field.

PETE FOX

Hank, Baker wants me to take your place.

HANK GREENBERG

Well, this is not between you and me, Pete.

PETE FOX

No, I guess not.

HANK GREENBERG

Then I guess I'll go inside and talk to them.

PETE FOX

Thanks, Hank

HANK GREENBERG VOICEOVER

It wasn't between me and Pete, I knew that. Pete had been a regular and now was a reserve so I didn't want to embarrass him in any way. I knew who I had to talk to. So I went right to the clubhouse and got dressed. Then I made a phone call.

HANK GREENBERG (on the phone)

Listen, Jack, I don't want to ever be embarrassed again. The season just started. It was a difficult ball out there for anybody. It dropped, and no matter who was playing left field or shortstop or third base, I've seen it happen a hundred times. But there was no reason to embarrass me by taking me out of that ballgame. If that's going to be the pattern, then the hell with it, I'm not going to play the outfield for you. You put me in the outfield, you take your chances that I can play outfield. Next time, I'm going to stay out there even if I get hit on the head with a fly ball. You better tell Del Baker he'd better not pull that trick again because there was no reason to do that. The next time he sends somebody out, I'm not going to get off the field.

HANK GREENBERG VOICEOVER

They listened to me because it didn't happen again the rest of the season. In time, I became a better-than-average left fielder with a strong throwing arm and a good sense of where to play the hitters. It was much easier than playing first base. There were fewer chances and I could concentrate on my hitting. That year, I batted .340, which is the highest average I ever attained in the Major Leagues. I also hit 41 homers and drove in 150 runs. We ended up battling Cleveland for the pennant.

EXT. BRIGGS STADIUM, DETROIT – DAY 1940

Pinky Higgins and Tommy Bridges are sitting in the upper deck of the stadium in left field looking through a hunting rifle telescopic lens.

PINKY HIGGINS

Look at this, Tommy, you can see the catcher down there.

TOMMY BRIDGES

Pretty interesting. This is better than one of
our hunting trips in the off-season.

PINKY HIGGINS

What's he doing now, Tommy?

TOMMY BRIDGES

He's giving the pitcher the signs. Wow, I can
tell what pitch they're going to throw.

PINKY HIGGINS

We'd better tell skip about this.

TOMMY BRIDGES

Yeah, someone can sit up here and relay
the signs down to the batter.

PINKY HIGGINS

Is it illegal, Tommy?

TOMMY BRIDGES

Don't think so and don't think anybody tried it before.

PINKY HIGGINS

Let's tell Baker.

HANK GREENBERG VOICEOVER

We tested the new system the next day. Pinky and Tommy,
however, were moved from the upper deck to the bullpen. A
guy was standing out at the center-field bullpen looking in and
another player was leaning against the fence and when he pulled
his right hand down, that meant it was a curveball, and if he kept
his right hand up, that meant it was a fastball. We used the system
for the rest of the season except against the Yankees. They had
a feeling something wasn't right, but never could prove it.

DEL BAKER

Our guest is in the upper deck today.

RUDY YORK

Fantastic, maybe I'll hit one out today

HANK GREENBERG

The best thing to have happened to us.

HANK GREENBERG VOICEOVER

And it was, too. We brought one of our minor league managers to Detroit, and he sat in the upper deck with a pair of binoculars. If he pulled his right hand down off the binoculars, it was a fastball. If he left it up there, it was a curveball. The players could easily spot him among all the spectators. Rudy and I had a field day. Our batting averages shot up, and we were hitting home runs for seventeen consecutive days for the month of September. Because of those signs, we won the 1940 pennant.

RADIO ANNOUNCER

Welcome, ladies and gentlemen, to the biggest series of the season, the Cleveland Indians and the Detroit Tigers. The Tigers have a two-game lead and need to win only one of the three games to take the pennant. Today's game will feature one of the best pitchers in the league, Bob Feller, against a rookie, Floyd Giebell.

HANK GREENBERG

Come on, Rudy, hit it out of here.

RUDY YORK

You got it.

RADIO ANNOUNCER

There's a ball to Rudy York. There's a man down on first, ladies and gentlemen, and here's the next pitch to York. (Crack of the bat) He hits it a long way to left field for a two-run homer and the Tigers now lead.

EXT. LEAGUE PARK, CLEVELAND – DAY 1940

HANK GREENBERG
You did it, Rudy, baby.

DEL BAKER
Nice shot, Rudy.

RUDY YORK
Thank our guest in the upper deck. Knowing what
he was going to throw really made me relax.

HANK GREENBERG
That's exactly how I feel about it, Rudy.

HANK GREENBERG VOICEOVER
With our new system, we won the 1940 pennant.
We were now favored in the World Series
against the much younger Cincinnati Reds.

RADIO ANNOUNCER
Hello, ladies and gentlemen, and welcome to the 1940 World
Series between the Cincinnati Reds and the Detroit Tigers.
Today's pitchers will be Paul Derringer and Bobo Newsom.

EXT. CROSLEY FIELD, CINCINNATI – DAY 1940

DEL BAKER
Let's go, Hank, get a hit.

HANK GREENBERG

You got it, skip.

RADIO ANNOUNCER

Here comes Hank Greenberg, ladies and gentlemen, for
the first time today. Here's the pitch from Derringer
and it's in there for a strike. Derringer in his windup and
the pitch… (crack of the bat) it's lined into left field for
a single. A good job of hitting by the Tiger slugger.

HANK GREENBERG (standing on first base)

What happened to our guest in the upper deck?

FIRST BASE COACH

He didn't show up.

HANK GREENBERG

Too bad, I could've used him.

HANK GREENBERG VOICEOVER

It's too bad we couldn't put our man out in centerfield
during the 1940 Series. But we were afraid somebody would
pick up on what he was doing and might lynch him. So we
had to do without the signs. I ended up going one for five
in that first game without the signs. I struck out twice,
grounded out and popped out after hitting that single.

RADIO ANNOUNCER

And so, ladies and gentlemen, Derringer was knocked
out in the second inning and Bobo Newsom went
on to pitch a seven to two Tiger victory.

Adam Pfeffer

HANK GREENBERG VOICEOVER

We went on to lose game two, five to three, and I was determined I would do my best to try to take game three.

EXT. BRIGGS STADIUM, DETROIT – DAY 1940

Hank Greenberg steps up to the plate.

HANK GREENBERG

Hello, gentlemen.

JIMMY WILSON, CINCINNATI CATCHER

We've been waiting for you.

HANK GREENBERG

Nice to be wanted.

UMPIRE

Ball one.

RADIO ANNOUNCER

And Greenberg takes ball one. Hank was saying before the game that he was partly responsible for the loss in game two against Bucky Walters. Here's the pitch to him, strike one. Hank said that if he had hit a better ball in the first inning, Walters would have been in deep trouble. Here's the pitch. It's belted to left-center and two runs are in. That will be a triple by Greenberg here in game three of the World Series.

HANK GREENBERG (smiling on third base)

That's the kind of shot we needed.

THIRD BASE COACH

Way to go, Hank.

HANK GREENBERG VOICEOVER

We ended up winning that game three, seven to four. But it wasn't the triple that won the game, it was a four-run seventh featuring two-run homers by York and Higgins. The main thing is that we won with the fourth game in Detroit.

RADIO ANNOUNCER

The Detroit Tigers lead the World Series, two games to one, as Paul Derringer goes up against Dizzy Trout. The Reds will try to tie the Series up with their ace on the mound.

EXT. BRIGGS STADIUM, DETROIT – DAY 1940

Hank Greenberg walks up to the plate swinging three bats. He tosses two of them away and smiles.

HANK GREENBERG

Hello, gentlemen.

The pitcher delivers the pitch.

UMPIRE

That's a strike.

HANK GREENBERG

Things are sure getting serious.

Adam Pfeffer

CINCINNATI CATCHER

Just get up there.

The pitcher delivers the pitch and there's a crack of the bat.

RADIO ANNOUNCER

There's a shot against the wall in left, and Greenberg
will pull in with a double and a run batted in. The Reds,
however, still lead this fourth game of the World Series.

HANK GREENBERG VOICEOVER

We had a hard time with Derringer. We lost the game, five to
two, and would come back with Bobo Newsom pitching the fifth
game. Newsom was unusually quiet in the clubhouse because his
father had died a few days before. He dedicated the game to him.

INT. TIGER LOCKER ROOM – DAY 1940

BOBO NEWSOM

My father was a great man. He only wanted the best for his family.
We tried giving him the best we had and hoped that was enough.
Well, now we're in the Series. That's all my father wanted. He
wanted us to win this more than anything else. So all I'm asking
is that you guys dig down deep inside and try to give the best
you've got and hope that it's enough. Not for me, but for my
old man who loved you guys more than anything. I know he's
rooting up there for us, so let's not disappoint him. Make my
father proud. Not only of me but of this whole organization.

The Tiger players cheer Bobo's words.

RADIO ANNOUNCER

Today's game is dedicated to Bobo Newsom's father, ladies and gentlemen, as Hammerin' Hank Greenberg steps up to the plate. Here's the pitch for a strike. Greenberg steps out of the box, swings his bat, and then moves back towards the plate. He knows how much this game means to Newsom, the Tiger pitcher. Here's the pitch and Greenberg wallops the ball to deep left-center. That ball is gone, ladies and gentlemen, for a three-run homer and a Tiger lead.

Hank Greenberg trots around the bases. When he gets to the Tiger dugout, Newsom jumps into his arms.

BOBO NEWSOM

You're the best, Hank, baby.

HANK GREENBERG

That was for your father, Bobo. I hope he's happy wherever he is.

BOBO NEWSOM

Oh, he's happy all right. Hank, you are the greatest hitter I've ever seen. Isn't he the greatest?

HANK GREENBERG

Thanks, Bobo.

BOBO NEWSOM

Did you see what my good friend, Hank, just did?

BILLY SULLIVAN

Your father must be very happy.

BOBO NEWSOM

Oh, he is all right. That Hank is the greatest. (crying)

Adam Pfeffer

HANK GREENBERG VOICEOVER

We went on to win that game, eight to nothing. Bobo pitched a three-hit shutout. My home run was one of three hits in five times at bat and I drove in four of the runs. For Bobo, it was the greatest game in his entire life. I feel good that I was a part of it.

BOBO NEWSOM (with tears)

You don't how much this game meant to me, guys.

BILLY SULLIVAN

We're all happy for you, Bobo.

BOBO NEWSOM

It was the toughest game I ever wanted to win.

CHARLIE GEHRINGER

Congratulations, Bobo.

BOBO NEWSOM

Bless all of you and bless you, Hank Greenberg.

HANK GREENBERG

Well, Bobo had won his game dedicated to his father and we were ahead three games to two in the Series. But it was not to be. Bucky Walters shut us out in game six, four to nothing. I went oh for three with one strikeout. Then with the Series tied three to three, Derringer went up against Bobo once again, who pitched on one day's rest. This time there was no magic and we lost, two to one, and lost the 1940 World Series four games to three. I could only muster two singles in four at bats in that seventh game. As a team, we were heartbroken. I remember coming back on that train from Cincinnati. We thought the season had been one, big disappointment.

INT. A TRAIN FROM CINCINNATI – NIGHT 1940

The Tiger players are passing around the bottle and drinking heavily.

BILLY SULLIVAN
Well, we tried.

CHARLIE GEHRINGER
Yeah, we tried all right.

BOBO NEWSOM
My father will understand.

RUDY YORK
Aw, Bobo's father will understand.

PINKY HIGGINS
I sure don't.

HANK GREENBERG
Look at you, mugs.

BILLY SULLIVAN
Bobo's father understands.

HANK GREENBERG
Well, he's about the only one.

CHARLIE GEHRINGER
We gave it our best shot.

Adam Pfeffer

HANK GREENBERG
But it wasn't enough.

RUDY YORK
We're just a bunch of bums.

HANK GREENBERG
Yeah, but there's always next year.

Taking a drink from the bottle.

HANK GREENBERG
And next year is usually better than this year.

PINKY HIGGINS
Isn't that the truth.

The bottle is being passed around the train.

BARNEY MCCOSKEY
What are the people of Detroit going to say?

HANK GREENBERG
They'll say, win it next year.

RUDY YORK
Aw, next year, we should have won it this year.

HANK GREENBERG
But we didn't.

PINKY HIGGINS
Hey, fellers, we're coming in to Detroit.

BILLY SULLIVAN
How does it look?

BOBO NEWSOM
I think I see some people.

HANK GREENBERG
Oh, they're out there all right.

PINKY HIGGINS
To stone us?

HANK GREENBERG
They don't look angry.

CHARLIE GEHRINGER
We'll know soon enough.

BARNEY MCCOSKEY
Are you getting out?

HANK GREENBERG
Well, we just can't stay in here.

CHARLIE GEHRINGER
It wouldn't be dignified.

PINKY HIGGINS
It wouldn't be right.

Adam Pfeffer

HANK GREENBERG
We have to be tough.

CHARLIE GEHRINGER
Yeah, what are they going to do to us, anyway?

BILLY SULLIVAN
I'm allergic to tar and feathers.

PINKY HIGGINS
Is there any way to sneak off without anyone seeing us?

HANK GREENBERG
If we sneak away, it will only make things worse.

RUDY YORK
They'll call us cowards.

PINKY HIGGINS
And they would be right.

HANK GREENBERG
We'd better face it like men.

PINKY HIGGINS
I was hoping you wouldn't say that.

The Tigers begin getting off the train. Some of them have to be helped along. There is quiet for a second and then the Tigers stand in the glow of the lights.

HANK GREENBERG
Before you say anything, we are truly...

Music starts playing. "Happy Days Are Here Again" fills the air.

HANK GREENBERG
I guess they're not angry.

CHARLIE GEHRINGER
They're here to cheer us.

PINKY HIGGINS
What a great city.

"Happy Days Are Here Again" plays on as the crowd waiting applauds.

BARNEY MCCOSKEY
What if we had won?

SOMEONE IN THE CROWD
Then you would have had a parade.

BARNEY MCCOSKEY
Gee, you people are nice.

HANK GREENBERG
To the city of Detroit.

BOBO NEWSOM
And to my father.

HANK GREENBERG
And to Bobo's father.

BOBO NEWSOM (singing)

Happy days are here again!

HANK GREENBERG VOICEOVER

It was a great welcome they gave us. We had been
defeated, but the city of Detroit made us feel as if it wasn't
so bad and that it was possible to gain redemption in the
future. Most of us never forgot that night in Detroit.

The fans and Tiger players celebrate in the streets.

INT. GREENBERG HOME – DAY 1940

RADIO ANNOUNCER

This just in: Hank Greenberg of the Detroit Tigers
has been named Most Valuable Player in the American
League, ahead of Bob Feller and Joe DiMaggio.

SARAH GREENBERG

He's still the best, my Henry.

DAVID GREENBERG

Some bum he turned out to be.

SARAH GREENBERG

Now Henry has already forgiven me for
saying the game was for bums.

DAVID GREENBERG

Really, Mama?

SARAH GREENBERG

Yes, of course.

HANK GREENBERG (speaking from the hallway)

Then you don't think I'm a bum and a freak?

SARAH GREENBERG

Henry, you're just big and tall.

HANK GREENBERG

Yes, mama, big and tall and not a freak.

SARAH GREENBERG

Oh, Henry, when are you going to get married?

HANK GREENBERG

When I find the right girl, mama.

SARAH GREENBERG

The right girl at that bum's game?

DAVID GREENBERG

Mama.

HANK GREENBERG

It may be a bum's game, but I'm not complaining.

SARAH GREENBERG

Oh, Henry, you know I didn't mean anything.

HANK GREENBERG

She didn't mean anything.

DAVID GREENBERG

Well, she shouldn't have said it.

SARAH GREENBERG

I know that Henry is the best player in that game.

HANK GREENBERG'

Even if it's a bum's game, right, mama?

SARAH GREENBERG

You'll leave the game after you find the right girl.

HANK GREENBERG

Maybe the right girl is a bum's daughter, eh, mama?

SARAH GREENBERG

Oh, Henry.

HANK GREENBERG

You think a rich man's daughter would
have anything to do with me?

SARAH GREENBERG

Of course, Henry.

HANK GREENBERG

You don't think I'm a freak?

SARAH GREENBERG

Just big and tall.

HANK GREENBERG

Okay, mama, big and tall.

DAVID GREENBERG

And Most Valuable Player.

HANK GREENBERG

Right, Pop.

HANK GREENBERG VOICEOVER

I came back to New York with my brother Joe, whose minor league season had ended. We were both watching the news very closely.

INT. DETROIT APARTMENT – DAY
1940 -- A WEEK EARLIER

JOE GREENBERG

Hitler is marching through the Low Countries and has taken France.

HANK GREENBERG

Now there's a draft in this country and everybody has to register.

JOE GREENBERG

Well, let's register in Geneva, New York, Hank.

HANK GREENBERG

Sounds as if it's as good a place as any.

Adam Pfeffer

HANK GREENBERG VOICEOVER

Well, we registered all right, Joe and I. When I got back from Hawaii, there were all kinds of photographers and newsmen at the dock. My draft number had been picked.

EXT. AT THE DOCK IN CALIFORNIA – DAY 1941

Reporters gather around Hank Greenberg.

REPORTER

You asking for a deferment, Hank?

HANK GREENBERG

No, I'm not asking for any kind of deferment. All I'm going to say is that when my number is up I'm going.

REPORTER

You going to fight, Hank?

HANK GREENBERG

What's all the fuss about? You'd think I was the only guy going into the army.

REPORTER

What about baseball, Hank?

HANK GREENBERG (smiling)

I'm in great shape.

REPORTER

You think the Tigers can repeat?

HANK GREENBERG

Yes, I think the Tigers can do it again. I guess most of the boys are signed for the season. That's swell. I'm leaving next week.

REPORTER

Are you signed for the season, Hank?

HANK GREENBERG

No, I'm not signed, but I won't have any trouble signing with them.

REPORTER

That's good to hear.

HANK GREENBERG

Well, that's all for now, boys.

HANK GREENBERG VOICEOVER

I was examined by the Detroit draft board during spring training in Lakeland, Florida. The doctor classified me a 4F because he said that I had supreme flat feet. I was pretty upset. The newspapers reported that I had bribed the doctor to put me in 4F. They made a big deal about it and it reminded me of how Jack Dempsey, the great boxer, was hounded during World War I. They made him a scapegoat and called him a shirker. Well, that was not me and it wasn't going to be me, I promised myself. So I got myself reexamined and declared fit. I was reclassified 1A and was scheduled for induction on May 7, 1941.

EXT. OUTSIDE BRIGGS STADIUM, DETROIT – DAY 1941

Reporters gather around Hank Greenberg.

HANK GREENBERG

It isn't as much of a sacrifice as it appears.

REPORTER

You going to ask for a deferment?

HANK GREENBERG

I never asked for a deferment. I made up my mind to go when I was called. My country comes first.

HANK GREENBERG VOICEOVER

They said things like Jews wouldn't fight for their country or that they were not well represented when it came to fighting. I was out to prove them wrong. I would fight for my country and be damned satisfied doing it.

RADIO ANNOUNCER

Here's Hammerin' Hank Greenberg coming to the plate, ladies and gentlemen. This is Hank's last game before he reports to Uncle Sam. He said he was hoping to hit home run 250 on his last at bat against Atley Donald and the New York Yankees.

EXT. BRIGGS STADIUM, DETROIT – DAY 1941

The Detroit Tigers are playing the New York Yankees.

UMPIRE

Ball one.

HANK GREENBERG

Wow, he's pretty wild out there.

BILL DICKEY

We're going to throw you nothing but fastballs, Hank.

UMPIRE

Ball two.

HANK GREENBERG

You trying to help me, Dickey?

BILL DICKEY

That's what it looks like.

HANK GREENBERG

You gotta be kidding.

BILL DICKEY

Look for a fastball.

HANK GREENBERG

Charity from the Yankees?

BILL DICKEY

Call it a goodwill gesture.

HANK GREENBERG

Yeah, right.

UMPIRE
Strike.

BILL DICKEY
Nothing but fastballs.

HANK GREENBERG
That's a good one, the Yankees are helping me.

BILL DICKEY
Think of it as a going away present.

HANK GREENBERG
Yeah, right.

RADIO ANNOUNCER
Here's the pitch, and Greenberg pops it up. Well, that's not the way he wanted to leave, but there's nothing he could do about it.

BILL DICKEY
I tried telling you.

HANK GREENBERG
I didn't believe you.

BILL DICKEY
Well, you got what you deserved.

HANK GREENBERG
Thanks, Dickey.

HANK GREENBERG VOICEOVER

I was given a going-away party that night. All of the Detroit players were there and most of the Yankees. They gave me a gold watch and then I left the next morning. I was inducted into the army at Fort Custer, Michigan. It was the Fifth Division, Second Infantry Anti-Tank Company. I didn't go through any basic training, but was put right into that unit. I really don't know why.

INT. UNITED STATES SENATE, WASHINGTON, D.C. – DAY 1941

SENATOR JOSHUA BAILEY OF NORTH CAROLINA

This Hank Greenberg is a fine example of young men inducted into the Army who had made a real sacrifice. Greenberg quit a $55,000-a-year job to serve his country at $21 a month. To my mind, he's a bigger hero than when he was knocking out home runs.

EXT. JACKSON STATE PRISON, MICHIGAN – DAY 1941

HANK GREENBERG VOICEOVER

I got requests to play baseball, but I declined them all because I would have to play on my free time. I did, however, get a request from Abe Bernstein to play in a game. Bernstein was head of the Purple Gang, which used to smuggle cases of liquor from Windsor, Canada, into Detroit during Prohibition. It seems Bernstein's brother, Joe, was convicted of killing someone and was given a life sentence at Jackson Prison. Abe said the warden

was a big baseball fan and asked me to play in an exhibition
game between the Fort Custer team and the prison team.
I agreed to play because Abe said it might help his brother.
Anyway, when I got there the only uniform that would fit me
was a prison uniform so I decided to play for the prison team.

HANK GREENBERG

All right, boys, let's get some runs.

PRISONER

We heard you were pretty good, show us how it's done.

HANK GREENBERG

That might be a good idea.

HANK GREENBERG walks up to the plate in a prison baseball
uniform.

HANK GREENBERG

Hello, gentlemen.

WARDEN (sitting in the stands)

Let's see some hitting, Hank.

HANK GREENBERG

No problem, warden.

UMPIRE

Ball.

HANK GREENBERG

Now don't walk me.

ARMY PITCHER

I'm not trying to walk you, Hank, but I'm not
going to lay it right in there, either.

HANK GREENBERG

That's fine with me.

The pitcher winds up and throws and there's the sound of the crack
of the bat.

PRISONER

Wow, would you look at that.

PRISONER

That's going clean out of the prison.

PRISONER

I'll get it! I'll get it!

WARDEN

That was some shot, Hank.

HANK GREENBERG

Just doing my part, warden.

WARDEN

Yes, Hank, very nice. (to his associate) Must have
been the longest home run in prison history.

HANK GREENBERG VOICEOVER

Well, I ended up collecting a double and two singles, along
with the homer, and the prison team won the game. When the
game was over, the warden took us all to the auditorium and

made a little presentation. I got a big hand from the prisoners and then we all went back to what we were doing. In August, Congress passed a law stating that men over 28 years old were not to be drafted. I was thirty and expected to be released but things dragged on until December 5, 1941. I was heading back to Detroit, hoping I could get ready for the 1942 season, when the Japanese bombed Pearl Harbor in Hawaii on December 7, 1941.

HANK GREENBERG is surrounded by reporters.

HANK GREENBERG

I'm going back into the Army in a few days
and forget baseball as a career.

REPORTER

You're the first Major Leaguer to enlist after Pearl Harbor.

HANK GREENBERG

Well, I'm going back in. We are in trouble and there
is only one thing to do – return to service.

REPORTER

Were you called back?

HANK GREENBERG

I have not been called back. I am going back of my own accord.

REPORTER

What about baseball?

HANK GREENBERG

Baseball is out the window as far as I'm concerned.
I don't know if I'll ever return to baseball.

REPORTER

When did you decide to reenlist?

HANK GREENBERG

When I heard about Pearl Harbor.

REPORTER

What did you do?

HANK GREENBERG

I said, that settles it for me, I'm reenlisting at once.

HANK GREENBERG VOICEOVER

I had enlisted in the air corps. I decided I was going to serve not in the infantry, but in the air force. I went in as a sergeant, which was my rank in the infantry. I reported to MacDill Field in Tampa, Florida and spent the spring waiting for an appointment to Officers Candidate School in Miami Beach. I went to Miami in July and spent twelve weeks there. I was finally commissioned a second lieutenant. I was assigned to the Flying Training Command in Fort Worth, Texas, in the Special Services. I didn't want to stay in Fort Worth, though. I ended up requesting a transfer and to be assigned overseas. I was finally assigned to the first group of B-29s to go overseas. We spent six months in India and then were ferried over to Burma into China.

EXT. AIR FORCE BASE, CHINA – DAY 1944

Hank Greenberg and General Blondie Saunders are driving in a jeep.

HANK GREENBERG
Everything looks good, general.

GENERAL SAUNDERS
All right, Hank, I'll take you to the control tower.

HANK GREENBERG
We're headed for Japan, general.

GENERAL SAUNDERS
Very good, Hank.

Hank Greenberg watches from the control tower. B-29s begin taking off. One of them suddenly goes over on its nose at the end of the air field. Hank Greenberg and Father Stack, the chaplain, start running for the plane.

HANK GREENBERG
We'd better hurry, padre.

As they are running, there's a sudden explosion about 30 yards away. It knocks them right into a drainage ditch alongside the rice patties. Pieces of metal float down from the sky.

HANK GREENBERG VOICEOVER
I couldn't talk or hear for a couple of days after that, but the main thing was nobody was killed. Some of the crew were pretty well banged up, but we all escaped with our lives. Anyway, I got recalled from China and came back to New York. It was the middle of 1944 and we were winning the war. I was reassigned to an outfit In New York. Talking to factory workers who had contributed to the war effort. I was finally discharged on June 14, 1945. The only time I had played baseball in all that time was at the prison. But now I would get ready to return to the Tigers and the Major Leagues. There was

only one thing that was more important at the time and that was Caral. I first met Caral Gimbel in 1944. My friend, Louis Marx, invited me for lunch in Greenwich, Connecticut.

EXT. GREENWICH, CONNECTICUT – DAY 1944

Hank Greenberg and his friend, Louis Marx, walk on the Gimbel estate.

HANK GREENBERG

This is some place, Lou.

LOUIS MARX

Everything money can buy, Hank. It's owned by Bernard Gimbel, president and principal owner of the Gimbel Brothers and Saks Fifth Avenue department stores.

HANK GREENBERG

Wow, he must be loaded.

LOUIS MARX

Well, all you have to do is look around you, my friend.

Hank suddenly looks and there's a woman on a horse riding through the estate. She almost runs him over.

HANK GREENBERG

Who the heck was that?

LOUIS MARX

That, my friend, is their daughter, Caral.

HANK GREENBERG

What a woman, she looked pretty comfortable up in that saddle.

LOUIS MARX

Almost too comfortable. Anyway, she wanted to meet you.

HANK GREENBERG

I think we already met, Lou.

As they laugh, the woman on the horse turns around and comes trotting back to them.

CARAL GIMBEL

Sorry about that. I didn't see you
gentlemen until the last moment.

HANK GREENBERG

Well, it's never too late.

She climbs down from the horse with Hank holding the reins.

CARAL GIMBEL

Hi, my name is Caral.

HANK GREENBERG

Hank Greenberg.

CARAL GIMBEL

The baseball star?

HANK GREENBERG

Only if that impresses you.

CARAL GIMBEL

Well, I really don't know much about the game.

HANK GREENBERG

Willing to learn?

CARAL GIMBEL

Of course, Mr. Greenberg, with the right teacher.

HANK GREENBERG

I bet you don't need teaching in too many areas.

CARAL GIMBEL

Quite right, but you would be surprised
what a good student I can be.

HANK GREENBERG

I'll bet.

CARAL GIMBEL

Is there anything I could teach you, Mr. Greenberg?

HANK GREENBERG

You'd be surprised.

CARAL GIMBEL

But you're such a big, handsome baseball hero.

HANK GREENBERG

You're not so bad yourself.

CARAL GIMBEL

Would you like to meet Popsie?

HANK GREENBERG

Yes, sure.

BERNARD GIMBEL

Hello, Hank, it's very nice to meet you.

HANK GREENBERG

You know who I am?

BERNARD GIMBEL

I'm a fan, I love hearing about all those home runs you've hit.

HANK GREENBERG

I can see you've hit one yourself, Mr. Gimbel.

CARAL GIMBEL (smiling)

Oh, he says that to all the girls.

BERNARD GIMBEL

I hope not.

HANK GREENBERG

You can rest assured, Mr. Gimbel. That was some home run.

They all laugh as they walk towards the house.

BERNARD GIMBEL

You're stationed in New York now?

HANK GREENBERG

Yes, for the time being, anyway.

BERNARD GIMBEL

Is there anything you'd like to see?

HANK GREENBERG (looking at Caral)

Yes, I can think of some things.

CARAL GIMBEL

Do you like horses?

HANK GREENBERG

No, I was kind of fond of who was sitting on the horse.

CARAL GIMBEL (smiling)

That's very kind of you, Mr. Greenberg.

HANK GREENBERG

I'm not really that nice.

CARAL GIMBEL

Oh, really?

HANK GREENBERG

No, but you seem to be different.

CARAL GIMBEL

In what way?

HANK GREENBERG

Well, you can handle a horse. I never met anyone who could handle a horse before.

CARAL GIMBEL

I can handle a lot of things, Mr. Greenberg.

HANK GREENBERG

I don't doubt it for a second.

BERNARD GIMBEL

You're only getting to know how good Caral is at many things.

HANK GREENBERG

I imagine so.

BERNARD GIMBEL

But now, I really think we should be heading to lunch.

HANK GREENBERG

Yes, Mr. Gimbel, it sounds like an excellent idea.

HANK GREENBERG VOICEOVER

We had a marvelous meal and I was really falling in love with Caral. I wanted to see her but really wasn't sure how to ask her.

HANK GREENBERG

Well, that was delicious.

CARAL GIMBEL

Better than those home-cooked meals you're used to?

HANK GREENBERG

That's pretty funny. I'm lucky I eat at all.

CARAL GIMBEL

There's nobody cooking for you?

HANK GREENBERG

That would be something.

CARAL GIMBEL

Of course, there would be a lot to cook.

HANK GREENBERG

Yes, playing ball gives me a huge appetite.

CARAL GIMBEL

A giant of a man.

HANK GREENBERG

Me?

CARAL GIMBEL

Yes, a good looking giant of a man.

HANK GREENBERG

You like giants?

CARAL GIMBEL

As long as they don't eat me.

HANK GREENBERG

Hey, you look like you taste pretty good.

Adam Pfeffer

CARAL GIMBEL (smiling)
You are a giant, aren't you?

HANK GREENBERG
As long as you like giants.

CARAL GIMBEL
I'd kind of like to find out.

HANK GREENBERG
So would I.

HANK GREENBERG VOICEOVER
Caral and I started seeing each other after that. We were happy and in love and I was ready to go back to baseball. She really didn't know anything about the game, but I decided I would try to teach her. But that would have to wait until after the baseball season.

RADIO ANNOUNCER
Nobody has attempted to resume baseball operations after so long a lapse. Hank Greenberg is returning to the Detroit Tiger lineup. There isn't a fan or a rival player who doesn't wish for Big Hank anything but the best of luck. He is the first of the stars to come back to the game and it will be interesting to see if everything returns to normal.

EXT. BRIGGS STADIUM, DETROIT – DAY 1945

Hank Greenberg strolls to the plate carrying three bats. He places two of them down and then steps into the batter's box. The Tigers are playing the Philadelphia A's.

HANK GREENBERG

Hello, gentlemen.

PHILADELPHIA CATCHER

Well, here comes a war hero.

HANK GREENBERG

Just looking for a hit.

PHILADELPHIA CATCHER

Yes, sir.

UMPIRE

Strike.

PHILADELPHIA CATCHER

Look alert, captain.

HANK GREENBERG

Just give me something to hit.

UMPIRE

Ball.

PHILADELPHIA CATCHER

Pick one you like, sir.

HANK GREENBERG

That's what I'm aiming to do.

RADIO ANNOUNCER

Here comes the pitch to Greenberg and it's swatted into left field. That's way back there. That's going to be gone, a home run for returning war veteran Hammerin' Hank Greenberg.

EXT. BRIGGS STADIUM, DETROIT, DUGOUT – DAY 1945

RUDY YORK

Way to go, Hank.

HANK GREENBERG

Boy, it felt good to hit that one.

RADIO ANNOUNCER

It had been 4 years, 1 month and 24 days since Greenberg had known the thrill of hitting a home run in a Major League ballpark and hearing the roar of the crowd.

HANK GREENBERG VOICEOVER

We ended up taking that game, nine to five. I played most of the second half of the season and wound up hitting .311. The batting championship went to George Stirnweiss of the Yankees, who hit .309. But I didn't have enough at bats to qualify. It was all right, the Tigers were fighting for the pennant. We went into St. Louis leading Washington by one game and needing a win in the final two games to clinch the pennant. If we lost both games, we'd end up in a tie with the Senators.

RADIO ANNOUNCER

The rain keeps falling here at Sportsman's Park for the final game of the 1945 season. The baselines are deep in mud and footing is slippery. But we have a ball game to play and it may decide who wins the 1945 American League pennant.

EXT. SPORTSMAN'S PARK, ST. LOUIS – DAY 1945

HANK GREENBERG

Come on, guys, let's get a rally going.

RUDY YORK

You got it, Hank.

RADIO ANNOUNCER

We go to the top of the ninth, the Browns leading this one, four to three. The afternoon light is fading, ladies and gentlemen, but there is a pennant at stake. Hub Walker will lead it off for the Tigers, pinch-hitting for Hal Newhouser, the pitcher.

UMPIRE

Strike.

HUB WALKER

Just like that one.

RADIO ANNOUNCER

Walker digging in. Here's the pitch and he rips a single into the outfield. Now the batter is Skeeter Webb. Webb bunts the ball. The first baseman picks it up and throws to second to get Walker. Oh, it hits Walker and both runners are safe. That's a big mistake, ladies and gentlemen. The next batter will be Eddie Mayo. Here's the pitch and Mayo puts down a perfect sacrifice bunt. He's thrown out at first, but the runners move up to second and third. The Browns now have to decide what to do with Doc Cramer, a left-handed batter. It looks like they're going to walk him and pitch to Greenberg.

EDDIE MAYO

Wait for your pitch, Hank.

RUDY YORK

Be patient up there.

RADIO ANNOUNCER

Here comes Hammerin' Hank Greenberg to the
plate with the bases loaded here in the ninth. Oh
my, what a way to end the season, folks.

HANK GREENBERG

Hello, gentlemen.

ST. LOUIS CATCHER

Nice to see you back, big Hank.

RADIO ANNOUNCER

Here's the wind-up, the pitch by Nelson Potter.

UMPIRE

Ball.

HANK GREENBERG

Now give me something good to hit.

RADIO ANNOUNCER

That's ball one to Greenberg here in the ninth. The
Browns lead it, four to three. St. Louis is hoping for
a double play. Here's the pitch to Greenberg.

There's a loud crack of the bat.

RADIO ANNOUNCER

It's a screaming line drive toward the left-field bleachers.
Greenberg's standing at home plate trying to will the ball fair.

HANK GREENBERG

Fair ball, fair ball.

UMPIRE

Fair ball.

HANK GREENBERG

All right!

RADIO ANNOUNCER

That's a home run for Hank Greenberg and the Tigers are about to win the pennant! A grand slam for Hammerin' Hank Greenberg puts the Tigers ahead here in the ninth, seven to four.

Hank Greenberg trots around the bases with all the Tiger players gathering at home plate.

RUDY YORK

You did it, Hank.

EDDIE MAYO

He did it all right.

HANK GREENBERG

All right, guys, we're going to the Series.

SKEETER WEBB

You know it, Hank.

The Tiger players gather around Hank Greenberg and celebrate at home plate.

Adam Pfeffer

HANK GREENBERG VOICEOVER

We won the game and the pennant and I was treated like a hero. I heard what the Washington players said after missing out on the Series: "Goddamn that dirty Jew bastard, he beat us again."

RADIO ANNOUNCER

Welcome, ladies and gentlemen, to the 1945 World Series featuring the Chicago Cubs and the Detroit Tigers. Today's pitching matchup is Hank Borowy for the Cubs and Hal Newhouser for the Tigers.

HANK GREENBERG VOICEOVER

That first game of the 1945 Series didn't go so well. We lost to Hank Borowy nine to nothing. I went oh for two, striking out once. But we came back in game two.

RADIO ANNOUNCER

Two on and two outs in the fifth as Hank Greenberg comes to the plate.

HANK GREENBERG

Hello, gentlemen.

CUB CATCHER

You'd better concentrate on the game.

HANK GREENBERG

You're right, my friend.

RADIO ANNOUNCER

Here's the pitch from Hank Wyse – that's ball one.

HANK GREENBERG

Give me something, Wyse.

RADIO ANNOUNCER

Wyse into his windup, and here's the pitch. It's a long fly ball
to deep left field. Oh my, ladies and gentlemen, Greenberg
has done it again. A big three-run homer to put the Tigers
out in front, four to one, in this second game of the 1945
World Series. What a shot by Hammerin' Hank.

Hank Greenberg trots around the bases and then heads for the
dugout.

SKEETER WEBB

Some shot, Hank.

HANK GREENBERG

Thanks, I really gave it a ride.

RUDY YORK

That's the way to poke it, Hank.

HANK GREENBERG VOICEOVER

We ended up winning that second game, but the Cubs came
back in game three. Claude Passeau pitched a one-hitter and
it was off to Wrigley Field. We won game four, four to one, to
tie up the Series at two. We wanted to win game five and take
an advantage in the Series. Hal Newhouser pitched for us.

RADIO ANNOUNCER

Here's Hammerin' Hank Greenberg coming to the plate, ladies
and gentlemen. He steps into the batter's box and waits for
the pitch. Down low, ball one. Borowy gets the ball back and
gets ready for his next pitch. Here's the windup, the pitch,
that's a smash to left field off the wall and Greenberg is in
with a double and run batted in. My oh my, a beautiful shot
by Greenberg to put the Tigers ahead in this World Series.

Adam Pfeffer

HANK GREENBERG VOICEOVER

We took game five, eight to four. I had three doubles and three runs batted in. We were now ahead in the Series, three games to two.

EXT. WRIGLEY FIELD, CHICAGO – DAY 1945

EDDIE MAYO

Let's go, Hank, get a hold of one.

HANK GREENBERG

I'll give it a shot.

RADIO ANNOUNCER

We're in the eighth and Hank Greenberg comes to the plate. The Cubs lead seven to six.

HANK GREENBERG

Hello, gentlemen.

CUB CATCHER

Tough game, Hank.

HANK GREENBERG

They all are, Mickey.

CUB CATCHER MICKEY LIVINGSTON

Yeah, don't I know it.

RADIO ANNOUNCER

The first pitch to Greenberg is low for a ball.

HANK GREENBERG

Couldn't do anything with that one.

RADIO ANNOUNCER

Here's the pitch and Greenberg sends it flying to left field. That's way back there, that's going to be gone for a home run and a tie ballgame. Hammerin' Hank Greenberg does it again, ladies and gentlemen.

Hank Greenberg trots around the bases.

DOC CRAMER

Way to knock it out, Hank.

RUDY YORK

Beautiful shot.

EDDIE MAYO

We're all tied up.

HANK GREENBERG

Thanks, guys.

RADIO ANNOUNCER

We're in the twelfth tied at seven with Stan Hack coming up for the Cubs. There's a shot into left field. Greenberg coming in for it, and it must have hit something, because it bounces over Greenberg's head to the wall. The winning run scores and the Cubs win this sixth game, eight to seven.

HANK GREENBERG VOICEOVER

What really happened is that the ball struck the head of the sprinkling system and bounced over my head. It was a freak play but the scorekeeper reversed his initial decision for the first time in World Series history and scored it as a hit instead of an error. I was pretty upset, anyway.

INT. WRIGLEY FIELD LOCKER ROOM – DAY 1945

Reporters are gathered around an angry Hank Greenberg.

REPORTER

What happened, Hank?

HANK GREENBERG

We play to win and I don't even care if they don't spell my name right. But a thing like that, losing that ball, should never happen. I never had a chance, it was three feet over my head.

REPORTER

What happened to you on that play?

HANK GREENBERG

What happened to me? What happened to you? Did you see the game?

HANK GREENBERG

The worst part about the game was that I injured my right wrist in the twelfth inning trying to hit a ball to right field. I told no one except the manager, Steve O'Neill.

We decided not to make any decision until the next day, the seventh game of the 1945 World Series.

INT. WRIGLEY FIELD LOCKER ROOM – DAY 1945

STEVE O'NEILL

How do you feel, Hank?

HANK GREENBERG

I think for the good of the team I better not play today.

STEVE O'NEILL

How bad is it?

HANK GREENBERG

I can't throw. I can't grip the bat properly, and with all that it means to the rest of the players I don't think I should be in the lineup.

STEVE O'NEILL

I don't know about that, Hank. I think we could suffer a severe morale loss if you're not in there.

HANK GREENBERG

But I'm not fit to play.

STEVE O'NEILL

We could use that to our advantage.

Adam Pfeffer

HANK GREENBERG

What do you mean?

STEVE O'NEILL

Well, think about it for a second. The Cubs
don't know anything about this.

HANK GREENBERG

Yeah, well, that's true.

STEVE O'NEILL

There are certain things we can do.

HANK GREENBERG

I'm listening, skip, I'm listening.

RADIO ANNOUNCER

The Tigers are here up in the first, ladies and gentlemen.
Skeeter Webb is on first with nobody out. Here's Eddie Mayo.

EXT. TIGER DUGOUT, WRIGLEY
FIELD, CHICAGO – DAY 1945

STEVE O'NEILL

Get ready, Hank.

HANK GREENBERG

No problem, skip.

RUDY YORK

Blast one out, Hank.

HANK GREENBERG

You got it.

RADIO ANNOUNCER

There's a base hit by Doc Cramer, scoring Webb.
The Tigers lead this seventh game and now
coming up is Hammerin' Hank Greenberg.

EXT. WRIGLEY FIELD, CHICAGO – DAY 1945

HANK GREENBERG

Hello, gentlemen.

CUB CATCHER

I know, give me something to hit.

HANK GREENBERG (smiling)

That's all we can hope for.

RADIO ANNOUNCER

There's two on and nobody out here in the first of
the seventh game. What a spot for Greenberg. The
Cub infield backs up as we wait for the pitch.

HANK GREENBERG tries to smile as he stands there at the plate,
but there is a lot of pain on his face as his mouth sags into a
grimacing frown.

HANK GREENBERG

Just pitch the ball.

RADIO ANNOUNCER

Here comes the pitch to Greenberg. He bunts it down
to first. Unbelievable, ladies and gentlemen, no one was
expecting that. Runners are now on second and third
with Roy Cullenbine coming up. No one in the park would
have guessed that the mighty Greenberg was bunting.

EXT. WRIGLEY FIELD, CHICAGO – DAY 1945

STEVE O'NEILL

That's the way to do it, Hank. One for the team.

HANK GREENBERG

I think we confused them.

STEVE O'NEILL

We'll see very shortly if the strategy paid off.

RADIO ANNOUNCER

Cullenbine trots down to first after the intentional walk to
load the bases. Here's Paul Richards coming up to bat.

STEVE O'NEILL

Come on, Paul, get a hold of one.

HANK GREENBERG (holding his injured wrist)

Let's go Paul, finish the job.

RADIO ANNOUNCER

Here's the pitch and it's ripped into center field. Three runs will score on the double by Richards and now the Tigers lead this seventh game, five to nothing.

HANK GREENBERG VOICEOVER

We went on to win that seventh game, nine to three, and won the 1945 World Series. It was an exciting World Series and we each got $8,000 plus for the winner's share. I played pretty well but all I kept thinking about was Caral. She stayed back in New York during the baseball season, and we kept in touch, but once the season was over, I immediately went to see her.

EXT. CONNECTICUT ESTATE – DAY 1945

Hank is walking on the Gimbel estate when he sees Caral, and smiling, runs to her and buries her in his arms.

HANK GREENBERG
Oh, it's so nice to see you again, darling.

CARAL GIMBEL
I heard about the sacrificial bunting.

HANK GREENBERG
No, sacrifice bunt, darling.

CARAL GIMBEL
Well, it won the World Series.

Adam Pfeffer

HANK GREENBERG

No, we just fooled them. I hurt my wrist.

CARAL GIMBEL

Are you all right, Hank?

HANK GREENBERG

It'll be fine in a few days.

CARAL GIMBEL

Popsie was so happy.

HANK GREENBERG

About what?

CARAL GIMBEL

About the Series, Hank, darling. We followed
you throughout the season.

HANK GREENBERG

Well, we won, darling.

CARAL GIMBEL

I know, darling.

HANK GREENBERG

Well, how are your horses?

CARAL GIMBEL

Do you want to go riding?

HANK GREENBERG

No, I just wanted to see you again.

CARAL GIMBEL

Oh, Hank, I was waiting the whole season for this day.

HANK GREENBERG

What day, darling?

CARAL GIMBEL

The day we could be together.

Hank hugs her and they passionately kiss.

HANK GREENBERG

I've been thinking about you the whole season.

CARAL GIMBEL

Me, too.

HANK GREENBERG

Let's make it official, Caral.

CARAL GIMBEL

What do you mean, Hank?

HANK GREENBERG

I mean, marry me, darling.

CARAL GIMBEL

Of course I will, darling.

Adam Pfeffer

HANK GREENBERG

Let's get married before the season starts again.

CARAL GIMBEL

Wait until Popsie hears about it.

HANK GREENBERG

He likes me?

CARAL GIMBEL

Are you kidding, Hank, he adores you.

HANK GREENBERG

Great, because I'm pretty fond of him, too.

CARAL GIMBEL

When does the season begin?

HANK GREENBERG

In April.

CARAL GIMBEL

Well, we can have a wedding in March, I guess.

HANK GREENBERG

I don't want anything too big.

CARAL GIMBEL

It doesn't have to be that big, Hank.

HANK GREENBERG

Just something nice and fast.

CARAL GIMBEL

But there will be people to think about.

HANK GREENBERG

Aw, forget them.

CARAL GIMBEL

What do you mean, Hank?

HANK GREENBERG

I mean I don't believe in big weddings.

CARAL GIMBEL

We'll make it smaller.

HANK GREENBERG

Our families don't mesh.

CARAL GIMBEL

What do you have in mind, Hank?

HANK GREENBERG

I don't know, but I know I want to marry you.

CARAL GIMBEL

Well, that's all that's important, darling.

HANK GREENBERG

You do want to get married, don't you?

CARAL GIMBEL

More than anything in the world, darling.

HANK GREENBERG

Good, then we worked it all out.

CARAL GIMBEL

What did we work out, darling?

HANK GREENBERG

That we want to get married.

CARAL GIMBEL

But we don't want a big wedding.

HANK GREENBERG

You see, everything's worked out.

CARAL GIMBEL

Yes, I guess so, darling, except for the important details.

HANK GREENBERG

Oh, those we can fill in later.

CARAL GIMBEL

Of course, darling.

HANK GREENBERG VOICEOVER

I really didn't want to tell Caral what I had planned. It involved heading to Florida in the car and then getting married there. My brother-in-law told me we could get married in Florida without waiting thirty days. It sounded perfect to me. The only thing left to do was convince Caral that it was the best thing to do under the circumstances. We wouldn't have a big wedding, but it would be a private wedding.

EXT. GIMBEL ESTATE, CONNECTICUT – DAY 1946

A car pulls up in front of the Gimbel mansion. Hank Greenberg is driving. He sees Caral walking nearby.

> HANK GREENBERG
> Get in, honey.

> CARAL GIMBEL
> Where are you taking me, Giant?

> HANK GREENBERG
> I thought we'd get married on the way to spring training.

> CARAL GIMBEL
> How romantic, honey. Shall we serve hot dogs?

> HANK GREENBERG
> Aw, Caral, do you want to get married or don't you?

> CARAL GIMBEL
> Just us, Hank?

> HANK GREENBERG
> Just us, honey. No families, no big weddings.

> CARAL GIMBEL
> You're serious.

> HANK GREENBERG
> You bet, you'll have a much better time down in Florida.

CARAL GIMBEL
That's where we're headed?

HANK GREENBERG
We'll get married in St. Augustine. That's
where the fountain of youth is.

CARAL GIMBEL
Sounds lovely.

HANK GREENBERG
It will be lovely, darling. Come on, just you and me.

CARAL GIMBEL
Can I at least take along a suitcase?

HANK GREENBERG
No problem, darling, I'll wait.

CARAL GIMBEL
Well, thank God for that.

HANK GREENBERG
You won't regret it, darling. We'll have fun.

CARAL GIMBEL
Okay, I'll be right down, darling.

HANK GREENBERG
Hurry if you can.

BERNARD GIMBEL

What seems to be going on here, Hank?

HANK GREENBERG

I'm taking your daughter with me to Florida
and we're going to be married.

BERNARD GIMBEL

I assume you want to avoid all the publicity.

HANK GREENBERG

Yes, sir, more than anything.

BERNARD GIMBEL

You know we could probably arrange something here,
but I guess you want to do this on your own.

HANK GREENBERG

Thanks, Mr. Gimbel.

BERNARD GIMBEL

Bernard, Hank. I think we'll get along with each other.

HANK GREENBERG

Yes, sir, I always thought so.

BERNARD GIMBEL

And how are the Tigers going to do?

HANK GREENBERG

It's hard to say. We look pretty good.

Adam Pfeffer

BERNARD GIMBEL

Are you going to play in the outfield?

HANK GREENBERG

No, they traded Rudy York, so I guess I'll be back at first base.

BERNARD GIMBEL

That's where you belong.

HANK GREENBERG

I guess so.

BERNARD GIMBEL

A big guy like you should definitely be at first.

HANK GREENBERG

Yes, sir.

BERNARD GIMBEL

It gives you a chance to concentrate on hitting home runs.

HANK GREENBERG

Yes, I guess so.

BERNARD GIMBEL

You've hit a lot of them, Hank.

HANK GREENBERG

Yes, sir.

BERNARD GIMBEL

I mean you almost had the record.

HANK GREENBERG

I came pretty close.

BERNARD GIMBEL

Why if they didn't stop pitching to you.

HANK GREENBERG

I'm not complaining.

BERNARD GIMBEL

Oh, yes, you believe it was all on the level.

HANK GREENBERG

Yes, sir, I do.

BERNARD GIMBEL

You know how they feel about us, Hank.

HANK GREENBERG

But they wouldn't rig the game.

BERNARD GIMBEL

I don't know about that. I know they switched
the last game to a bigger stadium.

HANK GREENBERG

Yes, sir.

BERNARD GIMBEL

And didn't you lead the league in walks that year?

HANK GREENBERG

Tied with Jimmie Foxx.

BERNARD GIMBEL

And only a few homers behind Ruth.

HANK GREENBERG

Yes, sir.

BERNARD GIMBEL

But you were ahead of him at one time.

HANK GREENBERG

I didn't get the pitches.

BERNARD GIMBEL

No, you didn't get the pitches. We never seem to.

HANK GREENBERG

We end up doing all right.

BERNARD GIMBEL

Because we work hard and we don't give up.

HANK GREENBERG

Yes, I guess.

BERNARD GIMBEL

They called you a lot of names at the ballpark, didn't they, Hank?

HANK GREENBERG

You know, the usual.

BERNARD GIMBEL

The usual? Was anybody else on the team insulted?

HANK GREENBERG

No, not really.

BERNARD GIMBEL

I thought so. It didn't get to you?

HANK GREENBERG

Aw, it was just a few names.

BERNARD GIMBEL

You're a good man, Henry Greenberg.

HANK GREENBERG

Thank you, Mr. Gimbel.

BERNARD GIMBEL

I don't know if Caral really appreciates
the kind of man she's getting.

HANK GREENBERG

I don't know.

BERNARD GIMBEL

Well, she'll know soon enough.

HANK GREENBERG

Thanks, Mr. Gimbel.

Caral Gimbel returns with a suitcase being brought out by one of
the servants.

Adam Pfeffer

CARAL GIMBEL

This should last a few days.

HANK GREENBERG

I hope so.

CARAL GIMBEL

Well, goodbye Popsie.

BERNARD GIMBEL

Bye, darling. You will call and tell us the good news?

CARAL GIMBEL

Of course.

BERNARD GIMBEL

Don't worry about anything. We'll release
a statement to the newspapers.

HANK GREENBERG

Thanks, Popsie.

BERNARD GIMBEL

Take care of her, Hank. Drive carefully.

HANK GREENBERG

You got it.

HANK GREENBERG VOICEOVER

As we drove away, I was convinced this was the best
thing for both of us. We would avoid the publicity, get
married, and then end up in Lakeland, where the Tigers

spent spring training. It would be better than anything else we could have thought of. At least I thought so.

EXT. BRUNSWICK, GEORGIA – DAY 1946

A car carrying Hank and Caral pulls into a parking lot.

HANK GREENBERG

We're about a hundred miles from St. Augustine, honey.

CARAL GIMBEL

It's very nice, Hank.

HANK GREENBERG

I think we should eat lunch and then try to make it to St. Augustine before sundown.

CARAL GIMBEL

Yes, a very good plan.

HANK GREENBERG

We'll be married by dusk.

CARAL GIMBEL

Caral Greenberg. I like it, Hank.

HANK GREENBERG

I hope so, honey.

CARAL GIMBEL

I never thought I'd be a baseball wife.

HANK GREENBERG

You'll enjoy it, I promise you.

CARAL GIMBEL

How many strikes do you get?

HANK GREENBERG

Three, honey, and four balls.

CARAL GIMBEL

And how many innings?

HANK GREENBERG

Nine, just like I told you.

CARAL GIMBEL

I'll get it straight before too long.

HANK GREENBERG

I know you will, honey. Come on, let's eat.

HANK GREENBERG VOICEOVER

We had lunch in Brunswick, Georgia, and then got back in the car and traveled down to St. Augustine. We got there about 4 pm and asked at the municipal court where we could get married. They told us we couldn't get married unless we waited thirty days and had blood tests and went through all the formalities. We were told the closest place we could be married without any formalities was Brunswick, Georgia, where we had lunch. Anyway, we went back to Brunswick and arrived around 6 or 7 pm. We found a justice of the peace, an elderly gent living on the outskirts of town, and he agreed to marry us. His wife was the witness.

EXT. JUSTICE OF THE PEACE, BRUNSWICK, GEORGIA – DAY 1946

JUSTICE OF THE PEACE

Do you take this woman to be your lawfully wedded wife?

HANK GREENBERG

I do.

JUSTICE OF THE PEACE

Do you take this man to be your lawfully wedded husband?

CARAL GIMBEL

I do.

JUSTICE OF THE PEACE

I pronounce you husband and wife. You may kiss the bride.

Hank and Caral kiss. She is wearing a dark blue suit, pearl necklace, pearl earrings and orchids. Hank is wearing a pepper and salt business suit.

JUSTICE'S WIFE

Sign this please.

HANK GREENBERG

Thank you. Here's one hundred dollars and thanks.

They get in the car, which has a iced bucket of champagne inside, and drive to a nearby restaurant.

HANK GREENBERG

Popsie probably released the announcement.

CARAL GREENBERG

What does it mean, Hank?

HANK GREENBERG

We'll probably see a newspaperman or two.

CARAL GREENBERG

The real story is where are we going to spend the night?

HANK GREENBERG

I'm working on that.

BRUNSWICK REPORTER

Excuse me, Mr. Greenberg, but can I get a
quote from you about your marriage?

HANK GREENBERG

No quotes right now. We still need a place to sleep.

BRUNSWICK REPORTER

I can get you a hotel. It's very quiet and no one will bother you.
I'll do it if you agree to give me a statement in the morning.

HANK GREENBERG

Where is the hotel?

BRUNSWICK REPORTER

Sea Island, right across the bay. It's a summer
hotel which is closed, but I know the owners
and can get you a room for the night.

HANK GREENBERG

You have a deal, son.

HANK GREENBERG VOICEOVER

I gave that reporter a story the following morning,
telling him I was looking forward to a long, happy
marriage with a lot of children. Then Caral and I
headed down to the Tigers' spring training camp in
Lakeland, Florida to get ready for the 1946 season.

RADIO ANNOUNCER

Hello, ladies and gentlemen, and welcome to Opening
Day of the 1946 baseball season. The Detroit Tigers
will start the season against the St. Louis Browns.

EXT. BRIGGS STADIUM, DETROIT – DAY 1946

Caral Greenberg is sitting in a box seat on the first base side of
home plate.

CARAL GREENBERG

Come on, Hank, hit the ball.

RADIO ANNOUNCER

We go to the fourth inning with the score tied, one to
one. Here comes Hank Greenberg to the plate.

Hank Greenberg swings three bats and then puts two of them aside.

CARAL GREENBERG

Woooooo, Hank, hit it far.

Hank Greenberg strolls to the plate.

HANK GREENBERG

Hello, gentlemen.

RADIO ANNOUNCER

There's a pitch down low, it's ball one to Greenberg.

CARAL GREENBERG (praying)

Please let Hank hit the ball.

RADIO ANNOUNCER

Here's the pitch to Greenberg and it's whacked into left field. That's way back there for a home run.

CARAL GREENBERG (standing up and cheering)

Yay, Hank.

Hank Greenberg trots around the bases and steps on home plate. He waves to Caral and then heads for the Tiger dugout.

CARAL GREENBERG

Oh, darling.

RADIO ANNOUNCER

Hammerin' Hank has done it again, ladies and gentlemen,

opening the new season the way the old one ended with
a home run off Nelson Potter and the Browns.

INT. BRIGGS STADIUM, DETROIT – DAY 1946

Caral runs into Hank's arms near the Tiger locker room.

CARAL GREENBERG

Oh, Hank, you were wonderful.

HANK GREENBERG

Thanks, darling, I hit it out just for you.

CARAL GREENBERG

Thank you, Giant, that was some hit.

HANK GREENBERG

It wasn't bad.

CARAL GREENBERG

Wasn't bad? You won the game, darling.

HANK GREENBERG

It's only one of many.

CARAL GREENBERG

How many home runs are you going to hit?

HANK GREENBERG

That's hard to say.

CARAL GREENBERG

Well, I want you to hit one for me every game.

HANK GREENBERG

I'd like to, but it's just not possible, darling.

CARAL GREENBERG

That's too bad. I was looking forward to it.

HANK GREENBERG

Well, we can celebrate when it does happen. How about that?

CARAL GREENBERG

Good idea, Giant.

HANK GREENBERG VOICEOVER

Caral learned more about baseball as the season continued. She attended every game and was my biggest supporter on and off the field. I was having a pretty good season, although I was only hitting .270. I was among the league leaders with 55 RBIs and second to Ted Williams with 22 home runs. And then the news came: I wasn't picked for the All-Star team in Boston.

INT. HOTEL ROOM – DAY 1946

HANK GREENBERG (throwing down the newspaper on the bed)
That does it. Those hateful son-of-a-bitches.

CARAL GREENBERG

What happened, Hank?

HANK GREENBERG

Aw, the all-star game. I wasn't picked this year.

CARAL GREENBERG

Not picked? Why your individual home run
percentage is best in the league.

HANK GREENBERG

It's the Jewish thing again.

CARAL GREENBERG

How can they overlook a slugging average like yours?

HANK GREENBERG

Honey? How do you know about my slugging average?

CARAL GREENBERG

I've been reading all the statistics, darling.

HANK GREENBERG

But why?

CARAL GREENBERG

Well, you know, I have to keep up with Hammerin' Hank.

HANK GREENBERG

Hammerin' Hank?

CARAL GREENBERG

That's what they call you, you know.

HANK GREENBERG

Yes, but I thought that was just at the ballpark.

CARAL GREENBERG

I am your wife and your partner, darling, I want
to know everything they call you.

HANK GREENBERG

Well, I don't know about everything.

CARAL GREENBERG

Everything, Hank, that's the key to a good marriage.

HANK GREENBERG

But if you knew some of the things they call me—

CARAL GREENBERG

The Jewish thing again?

HANK GREENBERG

You got it.

CARAL GREENBERG

Hank, we've got to do something about that.

HANK GREENBERG

You can't change the world, honey.

CARAL GREENBERG

So we sit there and take it?

HANK GREENBERG

Nothing else you can do.

CARAL GREENBERG

So no all-star game?

HANK GREENBERG

I'm sorry, honey, I was looking forward to taking you.

CARAL GREENBERG

Boston, this year.

HANK GREENBERG

Right.

CARAL GREENBERG

Geez, Hank, can't you threaten them or something?

HANK GREENBERG

Can't do it, honey, it's their world.

CARAL GREENBERG

Well, you're an all-star in my book.

HANK GREENBERG

Thanks, honey.

CARAL GREENBERG

No really, Hank, I've been following the games since Opening Day. You really do have the credentials to be the all-star first baseman.

HANK GREENBERG

Go tell the American League.

CARAL GREENBERG

Leading the league in home runs and runs batted in.

HANK GREENBERG

Yes, honey, everybody knows that.

CARAL GREENBERG

But still they didn't pick you?

HANK GREENBERG

We was robbed, honey, that's all there is to it.

CARAL GREENBERG

Yes, robbed.

HANK GREENBERG

Well, I'm not going to lose any sleep over it.

CARAL GREENBERG

But robbed, Hank.

HANK GREENBERG

Aw, it's just an all-star game, honey.

CARAL GREENBERG

Robbed.

HANK GREENBERG

I'll call the cops.

CARAL GREENBERG
But they are the cops, right, Hank?

HANK GREENBERG
Right, honey.

CARAL GREENBERG
But robbed, Hank.

HANK GREENBERG
Happens all the time, darling.

CARAL GREENBERG
Right.

INT. HOTEL LOBBY – DAY 1946

Newspaper reporters are gathered around Hank Greenberg.

REPORTER
What do you make of these rumors of your retirement in July?

HANK GREENBERG
I don't know, the way I figure it, if I'm so bad I ought to quit,
but there are a lot of other guys around in the same category.

REPORTER
What about the all-star game?

HANK GREENBERG

If it's because I wasn't picked for the all-star game, that's ridiculous. Isn't it baby stuff? Why should that make me quit? Sure, I felt bad about not making the team. I wanted to get in it and take my wife to Boston. We would have gotten a big thrill out of it. My last chance to make it. My wife never did see me in a big game like that. But it wouldn't make me quit.

REPORTER

What about next year?

HANK GREENBERG

I don't know, it all depends on how I feel. But I can tell you this: Baseball is my business and I want to stay in it. All that stuff about hooking me up with the department store business is kind of silly. As for playing ball, I feel I'm on borrowed time anyway, so I don't feel bad. I'm not the hitter I used to be.

REPORTER

Thanks, Hank.

HANK GREENBERG

I'm always glad to talk to you guys.

He sees Caral and smiles.

CARAL GREENBERG

Come on, Giant, let's go look at all the little people.

HANK GREENBERG

Even if I'm old and over the hill?

CARAL GREENBERG

Who said such things?

HANK GREENBERG

They want me to quit.

CARAL GREENBERG

You're not old, Hank, you're only 35.

HANK GREENBERG

Try telling them that.

CARAL GREENBERG

They're just jealous they can't play ball the way you can.

HANK GREENBERG

Maybe, but my legs are not like they used to be.

CARAL GREENBERG

Join the club, darling.

HANK GREENBERG

Honey, you don't care about the all-star game, do you?

CARAL GREENBERG

Not if you don't.

HANK GREENBERG

I mean they're trying to make a big thing about it.

CARAL GREENBERG

Just don't worry about what they say, honey,
just concentrate on playing ball.

Adam Pfeffer

HANK GREENBERG VOICEOVER

Caral was right, of course. I was only 35 but they tried to make me feel old. Well, my legs felt old, my reactions were not as good as they had been and I was a high-priced ballplayer who they expected more from than I was able to produce. But I was still only 35 years old. That didn't seem to matter to the crowds, the ballplayers or the reporters. To them, I was ancient. It was when the fans in Detroit began booing me that things began getting rough.

EXT. BRIGGS STADIUM, DETROIT – DAY 1946

The fans are booing as Hank Greenberg steps up to the plate.

CARAL GREENBERG
Come on, Hank, hit it out.

The pitcher pitches the ball and there's a loud crack of the bat.

CARAL GREENBERG
Yes, darling, you did it.

Hank Greenberg trots around the bases.

CARAL GREENBERG
Oh, thank goodness.

INT. OUTSIDE TIGER LOCKER ROOM – DAY 1946

Caral meets Hank outside of the locker room, smiling.

CARAL GREENBERG

You were terrific, darling.

HANK GREENBERG

It's just a baseball game, darling.

CARAL GREENBERG

What's wrong, Hank?

HANK GREENBERG

Well, there are more important things now.

CARAL GREENBERG

Like what?

HANK GREENBERG

Like you.

CARAL GREENBERG

Oh, Hank, I love you.

HANK GREENBERG

I love you, too.

CARAL GREENBERG

Let's go home and forget about the ballpark.

HANK GREENBERG

Good idea.

Adam Pfeffer

CARAL GREENBERG

You know that was your twenty-eighth homer of the season.

HANK GREENBERG

It's hard work, darling.

CARAL GREENBERG

Yes, I'm sure it is. You want to go home and relax?

HANK GREENBERG

Yes, Mrs. Greenberg, that's all I want to do.

CARAL GREENBERG

Mind if I tag along, Mr. Greenberg?

HANK GREENBERG

I wouldn't want it any other way.

HANK GREENBERG VOICEOVER

At the beginning of September I got into a hitting streak.
By September 16, I had hit 6 homers in six days, had
9 for the month, for a total of 37 for the season.

INT. GREENBERG HOME, DETROIT – DAY 1946

The Greenbergs are in the bedroom. Caral is sitting on the bed and
Hank standing nearby.

CARAL GREENBERG

So far this season you have hit more home runs than any
player in the Major Leagues except Ted Williams.

HANK GREENBERG (smiling)

Who told you that?

CARAL GREENBERG

It was in the newspaper, Giant.

HANK GREENBERG

What else was in there?

CARAL GREENBERG

Well, let's see. You have more homers than
the entire Chicago White Sox team.

HANK GREENBERG

Pretty good for an old man.

CARAL GREENBERG

You're darned right. The Old Man has hit more
homers than the next four Tigers – put together.

HANK GREENBERG

No wonder they think he should retire.

CARAL GREENBERG

Yes, of course. He has only driven in more than
twice as many runs as any other Tiger.

HANK GREENBERG

Well, I think he should hang them up.

Adam Pfeffer

CARAL GREENBERG
Hang what up, darling?

HANK GREENBERG
His spikes, honey.

CARAL GREENBERG
Yes, of course.

HANK GREENBERG
I'm old and over the hill.

CARAL GREENBERG
I'll be the judge of that.

HANK GREENBERG
Yes, of course, the little woman always knows.

CARAL GREENBERG
Well, this little woman knows.

HANK GREENBERG
Knows what?

CARAL GREENBERG
Knows that the Old Man is far from finished.

HANK GREENBERG
Nice to know somebody believes in me.

CARAL GREENBERG
Okay, now let's see what you've got, Old Man.

Hank and Caral smile and laugh, and then Hank gets on the bed and kisses her.

EXT. SPORTSMAN'S PARK, ST. LOUIS – DAY 1946

RADIO ANNOUNCER

Hank Greenberg up at bat, ladies and gentlemen, here
against the Browns. There's the pitch and it's belted
to deep left-centerfield, way back there, it's gone
for a home run, his forty-first of the season.

Caral Greenberg is sitting in a box seat near the Tiger visiting dugout.

CARAL GREENBERG (shouting as Hank
Greenberg trots around the bases)

Yes, darling, I love you.

Hank Greenberg steps on home plate and waves to Caral.

CARAL GREENBERG

Isn't he terrific? Nice shot, Old Man.

INT. HOTEL ROOM – DAY 1946

CARAL GREENBERG

Oh, Hank, you were great out there.

HANK GREENBERG

I still might have something left in the old bat.

CARAL GREENBERG

You surely do, my darling. They were cheering you.

HANK GREENBERG

The fans just want to see a good game.

CARAL GREENBERG

But they expect too much from you.

HANK GREENBERG

Well, they pay their money so they think they have the right.

CARAL GREENBERG

They don't realize the players are human beings.

HANK GREENBERG

They know but they have high expectations.

CARAL GREENBERG

Unrealistic, if you ask me.

HANK GREENBERG

Aw, they just want to win.

CARAL GREENBERG

Don't the players?

HANK GREENBERG

Of course, but we get paid whether we win or not.

CARAL GREENBERG

So that's it.

HANK GREENBERG

Pretty much. The fans pay their money and want to win and the players get paid to play the game and hopefully win.

CARAL GREENBERG

And what about you, Hank?

HANK GREENBERG

I get paid to hit home runs and knock in runs.

CARAL GREENBERG

And you like doing it, don't you?

HANK GREENBERG

Not as much as I like fooling around with you.

CARAL GREENBERG (smiling)

Oh, Hank.

EXT. BRIGGS STADIUM, DETROIT – DAY 1946

RADIO ANNOUNCER

Here's Hammerin' Hank coming up to bat.

Caral Greenberg is sitting in a box seat near the Tiger dugout.

Adam Pfeffer

CARAL GREENBERG
Come on, Hank, belt it.

An old man sitting next to her, looks at her in surprise.

CARAL GREENBERG (smiling)
Smack it, Hank. Whack it over the wall.

Caral looks back at the old man sitting next to her. Then there's a crack of the bat.

CARAL GREENBERG
All right, Hank, you smashed it.

The crowd is applauding as Hank Greenberg circles the bases.

CARAL GREENBERG
Good shot, Old Man.

INT. GREENBERG BEDROOM – NIGHT 1946

CARAL GREENBERG (reading from the newspaper)
In my opinion Greenberg's surge is one of baseball's greatest achievements. When you consider all the angles involved – the four years away from action, Greenberg's age, the handicap he faced in moving after such a power hitter as Williams has become.

HANK GREENBERG
Who is that?

CARAL GREENBERG

Grantland Rice.

HANK GREENBERG

I guess I had a pretty good year.

CARAL GREENBERG

Pretty good? Your home run total was nearly triple that of
your closest teammate in that department, Roy Cullenbine,
who had 15, and the RBIs were more than double the next
Tiger player in that category, Dick Wakefield, who had 59.

HANK GREENBERG

But they think I'm old.

CARAL GREENBERG

Old? You played in 144 games, second highest on the team.

HANK GREENBERG

We'll see what the team says.

CARAL GREENBERG

What can they say? You led the league with 44 home runs
and 127 runs batted in, ahead of the great Ted Williams.

HANK GREENBERG

If I'm washed up, a lot of guys in the majors
ought to go back to farming.

CARAL GREENBERG

That's the spirit, Old Man.

HANK GREENBERG

Tell me what else I did this year.

CARAL GREENBERG

Well, you were second in total bases and slugging average to Williams, but beat out old Ted in home run percentage.

HANK GREENBERG

Not too bad for an Old Man.

CARAL GREENBERG

Not too bad, indeed.

HANK GREENBERG

The only problem is we finished in second behind Boston.

CARAL GREENBERG

Well, you can't win it every year.

HANK GREENBERG

No, I guess not, but I feel like a winner anyway.

CARAL GREENBERG

Why is that?

HANK GREENBERG

I've got the best fan a man could hope for.

CARAL GREENBERG

I hope you mean me, Giant.

HANK GREENBERG (smiling)

There's no one else in that stadium I want to sleep with.

CARAL GREENBERG

I hope not.

INT. GREENBERG HOME – DAY 1947

HANK GREENBERG

Look out! We've got big trouble.

CARAL GREENBERG (anxious)

What happened, Hank?

HANK GREENBERG

Something in *The Sporting News*.

CARAL GREENBERG

Well, what is it?

HANK GREENBERG

There's a picture of me wearing a Yankees
uniform, and saying I want to play for them.

CARAL GREENBERG

Is it true?

HANK GREENBERG

Well, yes but there was a reason.

CARAL GREENBERG

What's the reason?

HANK GREENBERG

It happened four years ago when I was in the army in Fort Worth. I got a telegram from the War Department telling me to report to New York City to participate in a bond game. They were selling $100,000 worth of bonds for the game and they ordered me to play. Anyway, I went to New York and there was no uniform for me to wear, and we were at Yankee Stadium.

CARAL GREENBERG

So they gave you a Yankees uniform.

HANK GREENBERG

Right, honey. Then one of the newspapermen took a picture of me in the Yankee uniform.

CARAL GREENBERG

And now it runs in *The Sporting News*.

HANK GREENBERG

Yes, that's it, honey.

CARAL GREENBERG

You mean they ran that photograph after four years?

HANK GREENBERG

Yes, and now all of Detroit hates me.

CARAL GREENBERG

Just for wearing a stupid uniform, darling?

HANK GREENBERG

They think I'm an unappreciative slave.

CARAL GREENBERG

What are you going to do about it, Giant?

HANK GREENBERG

I'm going to show everybody the letter I wrote
to Mr. Briggs, the owner. I had written to him
asking for consideration as general manager.

CARAL GREENBERG

What does that mean?

HANK GREENBERG

It means I was asking to stay in Detroit, not leave it.

CARAL GREENBERG

Do you think they'll believe you?

HANK GREENBERG

They have to, darling.

CARAL GREENBERG

Why do they have to?

HANK GREENBERG

I spent my whole career here, I mean that
counts for something, doesn't it?

CARAL GREENBERG

Can't you go to another team?

Adam Pfeffer

HANK GREENBERG

You don't understand. I don't have the power to just go. They have to send me somewhere else.

CARAL GREENBERG

Well, why don't you ask them to send you?

HANK GREENBERG

Because I don't want to leave.

HANK GREENBERG VOICEOVER

But in Detroit, the newspapers started to write derogatory columns about me. The thing that angered everybody was that I no longer wanted to play in Detroit. When the letter came up, Mr. Briggs said he couldn't find the letter I had sent. Then he said even if he had received the letter, Henry Greenberg would never be considered for general manager because he didn't have the experience or the know-how. The Tiger owner added it was presumptuous of me to even apply for the job. Then I heard on the radio that I had been sent to the Pittsburgh Pirates in the National League on waivers. I couldn't believe it. Waivers.

INT. GREENBERG HOME – NIGHT 1947

CARAL GREENBERG (crying)

Oh, I'm so sorry, Hank.

HANK GREENBERG

It wasn't enough to get me off the team they had to ship me to a last-place club in the National League. They didn't even trade me. They didn't even get any players in exchange. No, they just send me away in the most insulting way possible – waivers.

CARAL GREENBERG

But how could it be, Hank? You were there for years.

HANK GREENBERG

Sixteen years and four pennants, the championship in 1945 and then leading the league in runs batted in and home runs last year. Then I get that telegram: (reading) The following telegram, dated January 18, 1947, was sent to "Henry Greenberg": This is to inform you that your contract has been assigned to the Pittsburgh club of the National League trust you will find your new connection a most profitable one. Signed Billy Evans. And I wanted to be that club's general manager.

CARAL GREENBERG

But you had such a good year.

HANK GREENBERG

Well, it's also a good year for prejudice and oppression. Do you know what Mr. Briggs, the owner, supposedly said to Billy Evans, the general manager? He said, we don't deserve that kind of treatment from a player with whom we have been overly generous. This is too much. Get rid of him!

CARAL GREENBERG

They can do that, Hank?

HANK GREENBERG

They can do anything they like. The players are like slaves who have no choice where they play. The Tigers thought of me as an unappreciative slave. Can you believe it?

Adam Pfeffer

CARAL GREENBERG

Don't get upset about it, Hank. You'll show
them the mistake they made.

HANK GREENBERG

Aw, I need a drink.

CARAL GREENBERG

That's not going to solve anything, Hank.

HANK GREENBERG

Well, it will help numb the pain I'm feeling.

CARAL GREENBERG

Oh, Hank.

HANK GREENBERG

A bum's game. My mother warned me. Just
a bunch of bums playing a game.

CARAL GREENBERG

No, Hank, don't.

HANK GREENBERG

And why not? I play my heart out for this team, do anything
they ask me to do even though I was successful at what I
had been doing and they sell me without a thought for the
rock- bottom waiver price of $10,000. No other players
involved. They just get rid of me because they feel like it.

CARAL GREENBERG

It happens to a lot of people, Hank.

HANK GREENBERG

Yeah, well, it doesn't happen to me. I was the best player on the team, and they sent me to another team, a last-place team, without so much as a thank you. What is the worth of a man, anyway? I mean, I'm a human being. I have feelings and emotions and the need to please and succeed, and they spat on everything and said, see you later. Thanks for nothing. What is the point, anyway?

CARAL GREENBERG

You'll come back, Hank, you're not really that old.

HANK GREENBERG

Come back? I've had enough. Ma was right. It is a bum's game. They treat you like a bum, and then if you hit, they pay you like a skilled bum, and then at the end, they get rid of you like a bum. A bum's game. Come back? I don't want to play this filthy game again. They find reasons to hate you, diminish you, and they get you in the end. No matter how you try to avoid being hated, they get you in the end.

Hank Greenberg throws his glass at the wall in disgust.

CARAL GREENBERG

Stop it, Hank, you've had a great career.

HANK GREENBERG

Yeah, great career, which ended with waivers to the worst team in the other league. Some great career.

CARAL GREENBERG

But you're very important to a lot of people.

HANK GREENBERG

What people?

Adam Pfeffer

CARAL GREENBERG

Your people.

HANK GREENBERG

My people? They will go on no matter what happens. They always have. Just what the point of it is, I really don't know.

CARAL GREENBERG

But there is a point to it, Hank. To keep the traditions going that have lasted thousands of years.

HANK GREENBERG

And they've been hated for thousands of years, too.

CARAL GREENBERG

But they go on, showing the world that they will not be defeated.

HANK GREENBERG

Aw, they don't talk about the ones who are defeated. The ones who put their lives on the line and then are sent down to defeat without a thought. They talk only about those who are successful in some way for a period of time that suddenly ends with their demise. I was successful for a short period of time and now I'm just an old man looking to start again.

CARAL GREENBERG

So start again, Hank.

HANK GREENBERG

There's no point, Caral. All I've got is you.

CARAL GREENBERG

Well, I'll go anywhere you go. If you go to Pittsburgh, I'll be there with you.

HANK GREENBERG

Thanks, darling, but I don't think I want to
play that bum's game anymore.

CARAL GREENBERG

But you were a Detroit Tiger for years.

HANK GREENBERG

Detroit Tigers? I hate that club. They thought they were
doing me a favor by paying me $75,000 a year. Well, I
worked my ass off for that money and then they just
toss me away. No, I think I'm done with baseball.

CARAL GREENBERG

You may regret it, Hank. You're only 36 years old. There's
still time to play. I mean you love the game and everything.

HANK GREENBERG

The only thing I love now is you, darling. Baseball has
taken as much as it has given me. I'm finished with it.

HANK GREENBERG VOICEOVER

I thought I was finished with it. That's what I told Roy Hamey,
the Pittsburgh general manager. The team had been bought
by four individuals, headed by Frank McKinney, a banker from
Indianapolis. The other three men were: Tom Johnson, John
Galbreath and Hollywood superstar Bing Crosby. I was told I was
helping them sell quite a few tickets because people believed the
Pirates were attempting to build a contending team. Then near
the end of January, Caral gave birth to Glenn, our first child. I
was wondering what I would be doing for an occupation when
I got a call from Galbreath. He wanted to have lunch with me.

INT. NEW YORK RESTAURANT – DAY 1947

Hank Greenberg and John Galbreath are sitting at a table in a New York restaurant.

JOHN GALBREATH

Just out of curiosity, I just wonder why you don't want to play.

HANK GREENBERG

Well, Mr. Galbreath, my allegiance has always been to the American League. I've played my whole career there , and I'd always thought I'd end my career in Detroit, and there's always been a bitter rivalry between the two leagues.

JOHN GALBREATH

Yes, I can understand that.

HANK GREENBERG

We never saw much of the teams in the other league except in the World Series and exhibition games. Naturally, in the World Series, the opposing team was your enemy, and there was no love lost between the leagues, especially from the standpoint of the National League.

JOHN GALBREATH

You mean because of the Yankees winning all the time?

HANK GREENBERG

Yes, they were always getting whipped in the World Series by the Yankees and the American League.

JOHN GALBREATH

Come to Pittsburgh, Hank, you'll enjoy it there.

HANK GREENBERG

An alien league not knowing anybody, and being in a strange city?

JOHN GALBREATH

You'll meet people.

HANK GREENBERG

I'm just not interested in playing anymore. The fans are going to expect a great deal from me since I hit 44 home runs last year and drove in close to 140 runs. Forbes Field is a big ballpark, and I'm not going to be able to hit that many home runs. I don't want to go there with the pressure of having to duplicate my season in Detroit and know that the fans are going to be disappointed.

JOHN GALBREATH

What are the distances in Detroit?

HANK GREENBERG

340 to the left-field line and the fence came straight across.

JOHN GALBREATH

Well, we'll do the same thing in Pittsburgh.

HANK GREENBERG

What do you mean?

JOHN GALBREATH

I mean we can build a bullpen out there and start the bullpen in from the wall and make it 340 feet from home plate and run it straight across, and then you would have the same target in Pittsburgh that you had in Detroit.

HANK GREENBERG

You know, Mr. Galbreath, I just don't want to play. I don't want to travel anymore. I can't travel on the trains. The berths are too small for me. Every time I go on a overnight trip, I wake up with a kink in my neck and I'm stiff and it's just not comfortable for me.

JOHN GALBREATH

That's no problem. We'll fly you. You can take a plane from city to city, and you won't have to worry about the trains.

HANK GREENBERG

I don't want any roommates. I'm married now, and I want to be by myself.

JOHN GALBREATH

We'll give you a suite. You don't have to have a roommate.

HANK GREENBERG

Mr. Galbreath, I'm never going to go through the shock of being traded or sold like a piece of merchandise like what just happened to me with Detroit. If you're willing to give me my outright release at the end of the season, I'll play one season for the Pirates.

JOHN GALBREATH

Okay, we'll do that. We'll give you your outright release. We'll agree to it.

HANK GREENBERG

What am I going to get paid?

JOHN GALBREATH

You'll get paid whatever you want.

HANK GREENBERG

How about $100,000?

You got it.

HANK GREENBERG VOICEOVER

I agreed to play one more season with the Pittsburgh
Pirates. I realized baseball was still in my blood and this was
a new challenge for me that I was looking forward to with
great anticipation. Then I went out and played squash and
developed bone chips. When the bone chips got stuck in
the joint, I couldn't straighten my arm and that's when the
problem started. I didn't want to tell the Pirates about it after
agreeing to all of my requests. So I played with the condition
throughout the 1947 season. But before heading to spring
training, I went to visit an old hero, the great Babe Ruth.

INT. BABE RUTH'S APARTMENT,
NEW YORK – DAY 1947

Babe Ruth has throat cancer as he sits in his apartment in his
robe and pajamas. He has a gravelly voice as he talks to Hank
Greenberg.

BABE RUTH

Hello, kid.

HANK GREENBERG

Hello, Babe. Can I get your autograph?

BABE RUTH

Sure, kid. (signing his name). Going to tell you something, Hank.
Hand me that bat. Now I'm going to show you the whole secret
of how I hit those home runs. Only fellow I ever told it to was

Lou Gehrig, when Lou first came up to the Yanks and Miller Huggins was trying to make a left-field hitter out of him.

Babe Ruth grips the bat with the little finger of his right hand extending down below the main surface of the handle and butt.

BABE RUTH (lightly swinging the bat)

Look, see how this grip makes your wrists break at the right moment? Throw the whole weight of the bat into the ball. With this grip, you've just got to follow through. Any other grip interferes with your follow-through.

HANK GREENBERG

That's pretty interesting, Babe. And nobody knew about it?

BABE RUTH

I kept it secret a long, long time.

HANK GREENBERG

How do you like what those Tigers did to me, Babe?

BABE RUTH

Well, I'm glad you finally signed up, Hank. A man's got to keep playing, if he's fit. Keep looking out for yourself. Keep your wind. That's everything.

HANK GREENBERG

Well, now I'm going to the National League, Babe.

BABE RUTH

You'll like the National League, especially the ballparks. I got a bum break when I went over there, but that was just accidental. You'll be okay. They'll curveball you a lot, and you'll find that they think a one-run lead is something nice to sit back and rest on. But otherwise it's the same baseball we played.

HANK GREENBERG

How do you know when it's time to quit, Babe?

BABE RUTH

Don't quit until every base is uphill. I played just a little too long… about a week or so. I should have quit that day in Pittsburgh – I was with the Braves, you know – when I hit three home runs and got gypped out of a fourth one by one of the Waners.

HANK GREENBERG

Yeah, Babe?

BABE RUTH

That should have been curtains. But I had promised old man Fuchs that I'd hang around for his Memorial Day crowd. Too bad—

HANK GREENBERG

Well, I guess I'll hang around for a little while longer, too, Babe.

BABE RUTH

That's the spirit, kid.

Babe Ruth and Hank Greenberg laugh together.

HANK GREENBERG VOICEOVER

That was the last I saw of the great Babe Ruth. He died in August of the following year. He was a nice man and he gave me a picture of himself that has hung in my house ever since.

EXT. WRIGLEY FIELD, CHICAGO – DAY 1947

RADIO ANNOUNCER

Welcome to Opening Day, ladies and gentlemen, as the Pittsburgh Pirates take on the Chicago Cubs here at Wrigley Field.

Caral Greenberg is sitting in box behind the Pirate dugout.

CARAL GREENBERG

Come on, Hank, knock it out.

RADIO ANNOUNCER

It's nothing-nothing here in the sixth inning, ladies and gentlemen, with Billy Cox on base and the batter is Hammerin' Hank Greenberg. He was purchased from Detroit during the winter.

Hank Greenberg walks to the plate swinging three bats. He tosses two of them away and then steps up to the plate.

HANK GREENBERG

Hello, gentlemen.

RADIO ANNOUNCER

Here's the pitch to Greenberg—

UMPIRE

Ball.

RADIO ANNOUNCER

Ball one. The aging slugger is making his debut as a National Leaguer.

UMPIRE

Strike.

RADIO ANNOUNCER

A one and one count to Greenberg here
in the sixth. Here's the pitch.

There's a loud crack of the bat.

RADIO ANNOUNCER

It's a line drive into the gap, and Billy Cox will
score. Greenberg will stop at second for a double
and the Pirates lead, one to nothing.

INT. OUTSIDE PIRATE LOCKER ROOM -- DAY 1947

Caral Greenberg sees Hank coming out of the locker room dressed
in a suit.

CARAL GREENBERG

Oh, Hank, you were wonderful.

HANK GREENBERG

Well, we're starting off okay.

CARAL GREENBERG

The Pirates are going to be the surprise
team of the National League.

HANK GREENBERG

Well, don't get too carried away.

CARAL GREENBERG
But the team looks pretty good.

HANK GREENBERG
Yeah, I guess.

CARAL GREENBERG
Oh, it will be a wonderful season, Hank,
I'm glad you decided to play.

HANK GREENBERG
I guess I am, too. The guys have been great to me.

CARAL GREENBERG
And what about the gals?

HANK GREENBERG
I'm just concentrating on my baseball, darling.

CARAL GREENBERG
Good, you do that, Giant.

HANK GREENBERG
I'll be a good boy.

EXT. WRIGLEY FIELD, CHICAGO – DAY 1947

RADIO ANNOUNCER
There's the pitch and Greenberg sends it screaming

to left field. That ball is gone for Hammerin' Hank's
first home run in the National League.

Hank Greenberg trots around the bases as the fans cheer.

CARAL GREENBERG
You're the best, Giant.

Hank Greenberg waves to her and then goes to the dugout, shaking
hands with his teammates.

HANK GREENBERG VOICEOVER
But there were bad days, too, in that season in Pittsburgh.
We were playing at Crosley Field against the Reds and I was
oh-for-seven in a doubleheader. I was pretty upset when I
came up to bat in the tenth inning of that second game.

EXT. CROSLEY FIELD, CINCINNATI – DAY 1947

Hank Greenberg steps up to the plate with the catcher Ray Mueller
watching him.

HANK GREENBERG
I haven't done anything today.

RAY MUELLER
Don't ask me to help you.

HANK GREENBERG
You wouldn't know, anyway.

Adam Pfeffer

Hank Greenberg pops the ball up to Mueller, who catches it.

HANK GREENBERG
Ridiculous.

Hank Greenberg smashes Mueller's catcher's mask and then hits it with his bat, sending it flying to the Pirate dugout. The mask is so bent, Mueller has to call timeout to get another mask.

RAY MUELLER
I didn't think an old man could do that much damage.

HANK GREENBERG
You're lucky it wasn't on your head.

Hank Greenberg walks away to the Pirate dugout.

RADIO ANNOUNCER
We go to the twelfth inning of today's doubleheader, ladies and gentlemen, and Hank Greenberg will be the batter.

RAY MUELLER
Oh, it's you again.

HANK GREENBERG
Been some day.

RAY MUELLER
It ain't over yet. You did some job on my mask.

HANK GREENBERG
Aw, so get another.

RAY MUELLER

Old man.

Hank Greenberg hits the ball and grounds out to the shortstop. Meanwhile, Mueller picks up Greenberg's bat and starts beating it in the ground.

HANK GREENBERG

Hey, that's my bat.

RAY MUELLER

Aw, so get another.

HANK GREENBERG

Give me that before you crack it.

There's suddenly a loud crack.

RAY MUELLER

Too late.

HANK GREENBERG

You dirty scrub.

RAY MUELLER

How's your day now, old man?

Ray Mueller laughs as Greenberg steps past the bat and heads for the dugout.

HANK GREENBERG VOICEOVER

One of the players I did get along with in Pittsburgh was Ralph Kiner. He was a young guy at the time with a beautiful swing, a great stance, and great power. But he got off to a bad start in 1947 and the Pittsburgh brass called me in to ask me if I thought they should send Ralph down to the minors.

INT. PITTSBURGH PIRATE OFFICES – DAY 1947

HANK GREENBERG

Here you have a guy who hit 23 home runs after he came out of the service and had led the league. He's young, how can you possibly think of sending him down to the minor leagues? It's ridiculous.

ROY HAMEY

Billy Herman thinks he should go down.

HANK GREENBERG

Well, the manager's not always right. I disagree. Keep Ralph Kiner with the team. I'll take him as a roommate. He and I will get along great, and I'm sure I can help him; I'm sure he'll put in a good performance.

HANK GREENBERG VOICEOVER

I was right about Kiner. He went on to hit 51 home runs that season to lead the National League. He went on to lead the National League in home runs seven times and was eventually elected to the Hall of Fame. But the Pittsburgh locker room wasn't a winning environment. Bing Crosby gave the team a record player, and a number of records. One of the favorite records was "Cigarettes and Whiskey and Wild, Wild Women." The team played the record after every game, blaring throughout the clubhouse. In Detroit, the clubhouse was dead silent after a loss. In Pittsburgh, the attitude was quite different.

Hank Greenberg and Ralph Kiner are eating on the roof garden of a hotel in St. Louis.

HANK GREENBERG VOICEOVER
One day Ralph and I were eating in St. Louis when we were joined by our catcher, Dixie Howell.

DIXIE HOWELL
What are you drinking, boys?

HANK GREENBERG (smiling)
A scotch and soda.

DIXIE HOWELL
Well, I think I'll have one. (To the waiter) Double scotch and soda.

HANK GREENBERG
You're playing today, Dixie.

DIXIE HOWELL
Aw, I'll be all right.

The waiter brings another glass with two empty glasses on the table.

HANK GREENBERG
Come on, Ralph, we'd better go.

DIXIE HOWELL
I'll see you out at the ballpark.

EXT. SPORTSMAN'S PARK, ST. LOUIS – DAY 1947

Dixie Howell is catching.

> ### BILLY HERMAN
> That's the sixth passed ball in the inning.

Hank Greenberg is laughing on first base.

> ### DIXIE HOWELL
> Come on, put it in there.

The ball hits Dixie square in the chest and knocks him down.

> ### DIXIE HOWELL (drunk)
> Nice pitch, baby.

Hank Greenberg is laughing on first base.

> ### HANK GREENBERG (talking to the runner on first)
> He's had one too many.

> ### HANK GREENBERG VOICEOVER

I'll never forget watching Dixie Howell trying to knock down Kirby Higbe's knuckleball with his chest protector. Everyone on the team knew what was going on except our manager, Billy Herman. How the inning ever ended, I don't really know. All I remember is Dixie dancing around in back of the plate trying to catch the knuckleball and drunk as anything. But there were real serious things happening in 1947. A man named Jackie Robinson was the center of attention around the National League. He was trying to become the first black player in Major League Baseball and end the color barrier that had existed for so long. I liked this Jackie Robinson and was determined to tell him so.

EXT. FORBES FIELD, PITTSBURGH – DAY 1947

Hank Greenberg is talking to a reporter on the field.

HANK GREENBERG
The more they ride him the more they will spur him on.
It threw me a lot when I first came up. I know how he
feels. They will keep needling Jackie, and he will react by
forcing himself to play over his head. I'll be awfully surprised
if I hear that Robinson fails to hit and hold his job.

REPORTER
Thanks, Hank.

HANK GREENBERG
Sure, no problem.

RADIO ANNOUNCER
Welcome to today's game between the Brooklyn
Dodgers and the Pittsburgh Pirates.

CARAL GREENBERG (from a nearby box seat)
Come on, Hank.

RADIO ANNOUNCER
And now coming up to bat is Jackie Robinson.

There's a ground ball and Jackie Robinson and Hank Greenberg
collide at first base.

HANK GREENBERG
Are you all right, Jackie?

JACKIE ROBINSON

I'm fine, thank you.

HANK GREENBERG VOICEOVER

That's how I first met the great Jackie Robinson. I talked
to him more the next time I saw him at first base.

Jackie Robinson hits a single to center field and runs to first base.

HANK GREENBERG

I forgot to ask you if you were hurt in that play.

JACKIE ROBINSON

No, I'm fine. How are you?

HANK GREENBERG

I'm doing fine. Stick in there. You're doing fine.
Keep your chin up. You'll be okay.

HANK GREENBERG VOICEOVER

I could hear in the background the voices of the Southern
ballplayers. Hey, coal mine, hey coal mine, hey you black coal
mine, we're going to get you! You ain't gonna play no baseball!
Jackie seemed not to hear it. But he heard it, I guess, just like I
heard what they screamed at me when I first came to the major
leagues. Jew bastard and kike son-of-a-bitch. With Jackie, you
heard the hated N-word. They called him everything, and some
of those things were being shouted by my teammates: We'll get
you next time at bat, you dumb black son of a bitch. We're going
to get you! I couldn't help but admire the man. He was like a
prince out there with his chin up and playing as hard as he could.
He was something to admire that afternoon in Pittsburgh.

Jackie Robinson smacks another single to center field and he runs
to first base.

HANK GREENBERG

Don't pay any attention to these Southern jockeys. They aren't worth anything as far as you're concerned.

JACKIE ROBINSON

Thank you. You're a classy guy, Hank Greenberg.

HANK GREENBERG

Not as classy as you, my friend. Would you like to go to dinner?

JACKIE ROBINSON

I'd love to go to dinner, but I shouldn't because it'll put you on the spot.

HANK GREENBERG

I don't care about that, Jackie.

JACKIE ROBINSON

No, you wouldn't, but a lot of guys would.

HANK GREENBERG

I know you're going to make it, my friend, because you're a winner all the way.

JACKIE ROBINSON

Thank you, my friend.

HANK GREENBERG VOICEOVER

We always were friends after that, even though he was in the National League and I went back to the American League as a club executive after that season. Times were changing, but very slowly.

EXT. FORBES FIELD, PITTSBURGH – DAY 1947

A ball is hit at Forbes Field to first base. The pitcher, Jim Bagby, goes to cover the bag and the ball goes through Hank Greenberg's legs.

JIM BAGBY

Hey, you big Jew son of a bitch, you make enough money to catch that kind of a ball.

HANK GREENBERG

I'm going to kill you after this game is over.

HANK GREENBERG VOICEOVER

When the game was over, Bagby was waiting for me in the locker room.

JIM BAGBY

Let's see what you've got, you big Jew.

HANK GREENBERG

Handle this, cracker.

Hank Greenberg throws a punch, but he's wearing his spikes and slips. As his feet flew out from under him, Greenberg is punched in the eye by Bagby. The players then separate them.

HANK GREENBERG VOICEOVER

As I said, things were getting better a little at a time. There was still a lot of prejudice and a lot of anger. I didn't care, I was ready to leave the baseball field and head into the front offices. The only thing that mattered to me was Caral. She made my final years in baseball tolerable.

CARAL GREENBERG

Are you going to retire, Giant?

HANK GREENBERG

Yes, I'm glad I ended when I did.

CARAL GREENBERG

You didn't do so badly, Hank.

HANK GREENBERG

Not by my standards, honey. I mean I only hit .249. That was my lowest batting average ever. But I did hit those 25 home runs for the Pirates, which was more than any other player on Pittsburgh ever hit. I promised that to John Galbreath and I'm glad I did it.

CARAL GREENBERG

Let's see. You played in 125 games, hit 25
home runs, and drove in 74 runs.

HANK GREENBERG

Not too bad for an old man.

CARAL GREENBERG

And you led the league in walks.

HANK GREENBERG

The only outstanding thing I was able to do for the Pirates.

CARAL GREENBERG

I know something outstanding you did, Hank.

HANK GREENBERG

What's that?

Adam Pfeffer

CARAL GREENBERG

You made me very happy.

HANK GREENBERG

That's all that matters to me, honey.

CARAL GREENBERG

What did the Pirates say?

HANK GREENBERG

Well, when I went to the office to say good-bye, Roy Hamey
begged me to come back for one more year. He said he
would pay me a $75,000 base salary, which is the highest
in the league. I told him I had it with baseball. My legs were
aching and I had a bad arm – those bone chips in the elbow
has given me problems all year. And I couldn't play on a losing
team. I couldn't carry a team anymore; I could hardly carry
myself. No, I told him, I'm through with active baseball.

CARAL GREENBERG

And you're okay with that?

HANK GREENBERG

Definitely, I don't want to play anymore.

CARAL GREENBERG

Good, we can settle down some place, Hank.

HANK GREENBERG

Yes, that's what I was thinking.

CARAL GREENBERG

It'll be good for the kids.

HANK GREENBERG

I can do anything I want to now.

CARAL GREENBERG

Why is that?

HANK GREENBERG

The Pirates gave me my unconditional release.

CARAL GREENBERG

That's something you won't be getting from me, darling.

HANK GREENBERG

No, my playing days aren't quite over.

CARAL GREENBERG

You said it, old man.

Hank and Caral Greenberg kiss.

HANK GREENBERG VOICEOVER

My name is Henry Benjamin Greenberg. I was elected to the Baseball Hall of Fame in 1956. My uniform number five was retired by the Detroit Tigers in 1983. I was an American League all-star from 1937 to 1940 and Most Valuable Player of the League in 1935 and 1940. After retiring from baseball, I became the general manager of the Cleveland Indians from 1948 to 1957 and remained in the front offices after that. My family was Jewish, but my religion has always been baseball.

THE END